"This devotional will help you discover] inside of you so that you can overcome . fulfill your God-given purpose."

—*Christine Caine*, *best-selling author, founder A21 & Propel Women*

"No one likes being stuck in life! That feeling of being trapped in failures, hardship, and sadness can be so debilitating. In this book, Sarah captures the very heart of that struggle and walks you to a place of victory in life. No matter where you are 'stuck' in your life, this devotional book will bless you. You will get the daily tools you need to untangle yourself and live free in Jesus."

—*Wendy Treat*, *Author and Co-Pastor of Christian Faith Center*

"Sarah beautifully illustrates that you and I were created to conquer in life and not just cope. She speaks with authority as one who has gone through many challenges and come out stronger. As you read (this devotional or each chapter), you will benefit from the encouragement and the rich practical insights she shares as if she was personally coaching you through the experience of becoming an overcome."

—*Colleen Rouse*, *Author and Founding Pastor of Victory Atlanta Church*

"Sarah has such a tender heart! Ever since she was a child, she's been pointing people to Jesus in a completely selfless way. You can clearly see her *heart to help* on display as she openly shares her very personal trials in the pages of her new devotional, *Advance*. In these extraordinary times, Sarah offers us a gentle *kick-in-the-seat-of-our-pants* and the encouragement we need to get ourselves unstuck and moving FORWARD again!"

—*Pastor Nicole Crank*, *Host of* The Nicole CrankShow, *Author of the* Hi God *devotional series, Speaker, Pastor, & Co-founder of* FaithChurch.com

"I highly recommend Sarah Wehrli's new devotional, *Advance: Living Unstuck and Moving Forward in Faith*—it is the perfect word for such a time as this! She is the real deal and writes from her years of experience in walking with the Lord. I love that this devo is loaded with Scriptural wisdom and I really enjoyed Sarah›s personal stories as they make each page come alive with personal and practical insights. If you are feeling stuck in *any* area of your life—you can move forward in faith and Sarah's book will definitely help you do it!"

—*Beth Jones*, Co-Pastor, Valley Family Church, Author, Reinvent: Start Fresh and Love Life, *and the* Getting a Grip on the Basics *series*, TV Host, The Basics With Beth

"Like a timely roadmap with practical, God-breathed instructions, my friend, Sarah Wehrli, shows us how to let go of whatever holds us back and plow through to repeated victories. You CAN break through the blur of resistance with hope for the road ahead!"

—*Lynette Lewis*, TEDx speaker, pastor's wife, author of Climbing the Ladder in Stilettos

"Sarah Wehrli brings a practical devotional, written during the Covid-19 pandemic, that, in 30 days, will help you break free from the clutches of spiritual prisons and move forward. A fluid reading with a strong foundation in the word, inspired by personal discoveries, and with a practical step by step in every chapter to take you to a new place. I hope this book is as encouraging for you as it was for me."

—*Priscila Rodovalho Cunha*, Pastor of Igreja Sara Nossa Terra Church, Brazil

"This authored and timeless book, ADVANCE, couldn't have come at a more appropriate time in the lives of many. On this earth, the natural predisposition of life as we know it, demands or necessitates that each one of us harnesses within ourselves the will to press on—and this book gives a guide to do just that. Is it fatality, loss or death, disillusionment, rejection or regret? The words written on these pages are a reviver to a better (normal) life."

—*Jessica Kayanja*, Co- Pastor Miracle Centre Cathedral, Uganda

"Pulling from the deep well of her own experiences of planting a church in another city and on serving the Lord in the foreign mission field, Sarah brings a message of spiritual motivation that is sure to pull you out of any mundane mire you may be stuck in."

—*Carla Strombeck Hornung*, Pastor of Agua Viva Church, Peru

"Are you ready to take your faith to another level? This 30-day devotional is sure to strengthen and motivate you to ADVANCE in your faith because the author herself embodies what advancing in God means. The title of this devotional is so much more than a title, it is the true heart and spirit of the author. We are living in such a significant time where our choice to advance in God is of upmost importance. Open wide your heart, as you are called to not just exist but to advance!"

—*Hannah Ouellette, Co-pastor of Thrive Church Denver*

"Sarah is a phenomenal wife, mom, friend, and leader. Her heart to serve and see people come to know Jesus is inspiring! I know there are so many people on the other side of this incredible devotional who will be encouraged and empowered to move forward and become all that God has called them to be."

—*Oneka Mcclellan, Co-Pastor of Shoreline City Church Dallas*

Copyright © 2020 by Sarah Wehrli

Published by Four Rivers Media

All rights reserved. No portion of this book may be reproduced, stored in a retrieval system, or transmitted in any form or by any means—electronic, mechanical, photocopy, recording, scanning, or other—except for brief quotations in critical reviews or articles, without prior written permission of the author.

Scripture quotations marked KJV are taken from the King James Version of the Bible. Public domain. | Scripture quotations marked NIV are taken from the Holy Bible, New International Version®, NIV®. Copyright © 1973, 1978, 1984, 2011 by Biblica, Inc.™ Used by permission of Zondervan. All rights reserved worldwide. www.zondervan.com. The "NIV" and "New International Version" are trademarks registered in the United States Patent and Trademark Office by Biblica, Inc.™ | Scripture quotations marked NKJV are taken from the New King James Version®. Copyright © 1982 by Thomas Nelson. Used by permission. All rights reserved. | Scripture quotations marked NLT are taken from the Holy Bible, New Living Translation, copyright © 1996, 2004, 2015 by Tyndale House Foundation. Used by permission of Tyndale House Publishers, Inc., Carol Stream, Illinois 60188. All rights reserved. | Scripture quotations marked MSG are taken from THE MESSAGE, copyright © 1993, 1994, 1995, 1996, 2000, 2001, 2002 by Eugene H. Peterson. Used by permission of NavPress. All rights reserved. Represented by Tyndale House Publishers, Inc. | Scripture quotations marked AMP taken from The Amplified Bible®, Copyright © 1960, 1962, 1963, 1968, 1971, 1972, 1973, 1975, 1977, 1995 by The Lockman Foundation. Used by permission. www.Lockman.org. | Scripture quotations marked AMPC are taken from the Amplified Bible, Classic Edition®. All rights reserved. For Permission To Quote information visit http://www.lockman.org/. The "Amplified" trademark is registered in the United States Patent and Trademark Office by The Lockman Foundation. Use of this trademark requires the permission of The Lockman Foundation.

For foreign and subsidiary rights, contact the author.

Cover design by: Sara Young

ISBN: 978-1-950718-76-4   1 2 3 4 5 6 7 8 9 10

Printed in the United States of America

30 DAY DEVOTIONAL

advance

LIVING UNSTUCK
AND MOVING
FORWARD IN FAITH

SARAH WEHRLI

FO
UR

CONTENTS

A Note From The Author

God placed the message of *ADVANCE* on my heart during the COVID-19 pandemic that halted life in the spring of 2020. Suddenly, all plans evaporated, and many people were stuck. Stuck physically as experts implemented plans to contain the virus, but also stuck spiritually.

I saw parallels of how being stuck in the natural can lead to spiritual stagnation, and I knew that I needed to share this message of hope—that you can break free and move forward despite your circumstances. This truth is universal and not limited to a specific time. Rather, it is applicable to anyone at any time when you might feel stuck and in need of encouragement to move forward in faith.

In this devotional, you'll discover biblical principles and practical steps on how to break free from anything that has been holding you back and move forward in faith towards the new things God has for you. Within each devotional, there are questions that will help you process and apply what you are learning. I've also created video lessons that you can access to complement your study. Over these next 30 days, as we spend time together in this devotional, and as you are seeking God in the word and in prayer, I pray that you would be filled with hope knowing that God can turn what the enemy meant for evil around for your good. Your best days are not behind you—they are in front of you. This is your time to advance!

Cheering you on,
Sarah

one

Break Free and Move Forward

You may feel stuck in the natural, isolated, or overwhelmed with all that is going on in our world, but I want to encourage you that you don't have to live stuck in your heart and mind, even if you do feel stuck in the natural. You can still advance in your walk with God and in the purpose He has for your life! You can live unstuck and move forward in faith.

In Deuteronomy 1:6-8, the Bible tells of a time when the children of Israel were moving toward the promised land, but they got stuck. They had just come out of Egypt, out of bondage, and they were free, but they were still wandering in the wilderness.

The Lord spoke to them through Moses at this point and said, "You have stayed long enough at this mountain. Break camp and advance to the hill country of the Amorites ... see, I have given you this land. Go in and take possession of the land the Lord swore He would give to your fathers...and to their descendants after them'" (Deuteronomy 1: 6-7a, 8 NIV).

Here is the big picture of this story: they had been set free, but they were still wandering and stuck at a mountain, which was keeping them from their promised land. They made what should have been an 11 day journey a 40-year journey. They were not moving forward. Isn't this true for us sometimes? We can get stuck in our minds and hearts because of our own mountains, whether they be mountains of fear, rejection, disappointment, discouragement, grief, or anxiety. We've been promised freedom, peace, purpose, and joy but through our circumstances we get stuck in fear, bitterness, depression, shame, and wrong mindsets.

Have you ever been there? Stuck in pain? Bitterness? Comparison? Fear? Shame? Regret? You want to move forward, but don't know how? I have. I've been there when, at times, I felt like I was circling a mountain. I had to make a choice with every mountain I faced, if I was going to get stuck or move forward trusting God's plan for my life.

Nineteen years ago, I wondered how I would get over a broken heart after having to break off my engagement one week before my wedding.

Twelve years ago, I wondered how I would get over the mountain of fear when God spoke to my husband and me about moving to the mission field with our two babies.

Eleven years ago, I faced a mountain of fear when my son got very ill on the mission field and I was standing in faith for his life.

Ten years ago, when my dad passed, I wondered how I would get past that mountain of grief and fear of the future.

Nine years ago, I wondered how God would provide for the dream in my heart to build children's rescue homes all over the world.

Six years ago, when God called us to plant a church, I had to get over the mountain of fear to step out in faith and obey, trusting He would provide.

Other times, when I experienced hurt and betrayal from those who had been close to us, I had to get beyond the mountain of pain and bitterness.

Every one of us face mountains at different times in our lives. For you, it could be the mountain of fear, lack, sickness, grief, rejection, bitterness, disappointment, or shame. It may be related to loved ones, or to finances.

The good news is that there are greater things ahead than anything you leave behind! God's plans for you are good. The promises in His word are still true. He will give you the grace to move forward in whatever area you feel stuck in because God takes us from faith to faith, strength to strength, and glory to glory! He has more in store for you! There are some steps we must take in order to advance.

Let Go

First, we must let go of something. In Deuteronomy 1:7 (NIV), they say "break camp", which can be translated as "to break free from." We all have to let go of something in order to take hold of the new things God has for us!

Paul said in Philippians 3:13b-14 (NIV), "but one thing I do: forgetting what is behind and straining toward what is ahead, I press on toward the goal to win the prize for which God has called me heavenward in Christ Jesus."

In the natural, this is something we do all the time. For example, I clean out my fridge regularly. I throw out the expired items to make room for fresh, new healthy food for my family. The same is true in the spiritual realm. We have to let go of things that are not working and keeping us stuck. We have to make room in our hearts for God to bring the new things He has for us and has promised to us.

Think about the things you might need to let go of that are holding you back. My prayer is that as you immerse yourself in this devotional, the Lord will show you what those are and give you the strength to release those things and move forward in purpose.

Magnify Him

The second way we advance is to magnify Him! To magnify means to focus on something or zoom in. Just as you would use a magnifying glass to zoom in on something, when we are facing a mountain, we must zoom in on the greatness of God. Whatever you focus on becomes big in your eyes. When we magnify fear, it can overwhelm us; when we magnify God and what His word says, faith rises up in our lives! Our perspective changes when we begin to focus on the greatness of God and meditate on His faithfulness.

Psalm 77:11-12 (NIV) says, "I will remember the deeds of the Lord, yes I will remember your miracles of long ago. I will consider all your works and meditate on all your mighty deeds." This is something that the children of Israel forgot. God had done incredible things for them: He brought them out of bondage, parted the Red Sea, fed them by raining manna down from heaven, gave them water out of a rock, and led them by a cloud during the day and fire by night. He had done miraculous things, but they still complained and didn't believe in God's ability to give them the new land. Even though Caleb and Joshua said, "the Lord will go before us—He will fight for us," the majority didn't believe, so they wandered around the desert and never went in to possess all God had promised.

Our perspective changes when we begin to focus on the greatness of God and meditate on His faithfulness.

When we remember the good things God has done in the past, it builds our faith for the future. Daily, I thank God for miracles He has done in the past and then speak His word over my life, children, marriage, family, and future.

I challenge you to think about what you have been magnifying. Make a list of all the good things God has done for you in the past to build your faith for the future. Then, thank Him out loud for all He has done. Psalm 34:3 (NKJV) says, "Oh, magnify the Lord with me, and let us exalt His name together!" As you remember God's faithfulness from the past, magnify Him, and then pray His word over that situation, things change. You may not see it change immediately, but you know He is working. You change!

Take Action

The third way we advance is to take action. For the children of Israel, they had to take steps of faith toward the promised land God had given them. They took ground and territory for the kingdom of God. You may be wondering how you can take action and step out in faith. One way you can take action is by completing this devotional prayerfully, because we win the battle on the inside before we see the victory on the outside. Part of taking action is choosing to set aside a part of your day to renew your mind with the Word—with who God is and what His Word says about you.

At some point, we have to say, "I'm not going to stay at this mountain of fear, hurt, complaining, excuses, or bitterness—I'm moving forward in God! God, I trust You, You love me, Your plans for me are good, and You are working all things together for my good. I commit these things to You and believe that You are working!" As you move forward into the new things God has, you'll receive fresh vision, fresh strength, fresh strategy, and fresh faith.

Now, let's advance!

Lord, give me the grace to let go of those things that are holding me back, magnify You and Your promises, and take action in the things You show me. Thank you, God, that You've promised me freedom and I pray that I experience the freedom and victory You have provided for me. Please bring peace over my heart and mind in Jesus' name. Amen.

1) What are some ways that you can magnify God?

_____

_____

_____

2) Memory list: share here the times God has brought you through a major challenge.

_____

_____

_____

3) What are some promises of God that you can stand on in the challenges you currently face?

_____

_____

_____

two

Fear →» Faith

We are all human and we all feel fear from time to time: fear of the future, fear of failure, fear of lack, fear of sickness, or fear of what people think. There are many kinds of fears. In this world, fear is all around us. There are severe hardships locally and globally, and many face real fears like losing a job, sickness, hunger, pain, loneliness, abuse, or fill in the blank for your situation. At the same time, that doesn't mean we have to allow the fear to rule our hearts and minds by dictating our decisions. We need to remember that fear is a spirit. With God's help, you can break free from the spirit of fear and move forward in faith!

2 Timothy 1:7 (NKJV) reassures us that, "God has not given us a spirit of fear but of power and of love and of a sound mind." This does not mean that you won't feel fear, since we are still human. It does mean that you don't have to let the spirit of fear rule you. All throughout Scripture, the phrase, "do not fear," is mentioned 365 times. Coincidentally, that's a daily reminder to not let fear rule your life.

When you meditate on God's love for you and cast your cares on the Lord, peace comes, faith rises, and fear vanishes.

In Romans 8:15 (NIV), we are reminded that, "the Spirit you received does not make you slaves, so that you live in fear again; rather the Spirit you received brought about your adoption to sonship. And by him we cry, 'Abba Father!'" The beauty of this Scripture is that we are officially named as sons and daughters of God. He goes on to share the following encouragement:

What, then, shall we say in response to these things? If God is for us, who can be against us? He who did not spare his own Son, but gave him up for us all—how will he not also, along with him, graciously give us all things? Who will bring any charge against those whom God has chosen? It is God who justifies. Who then is the one who condemns? No one. Christ Jesus who died—more than that, who was raised to life—is at the right hand of God and is also interceding for us. Who shall separate us from the love of Christ? Shall trouble or hardship or persecution or famine or nakedness or danger or sword? No, in all these things we are more than conquerors through him who loved us. For I am convinced that neither death nor life, neither angels nor demons, neither the present nor the future, nor any powers, neither height nor depth, nor anything else in all creation, will be able to separate us from the love of God that is in Christ Jesus our Lord (Romans 8:31-35, 37-39 NIV).

Part of our inheritance as children of God is that we don't have to let fear rule us!

When I was 16 years old on a mission trip in Ghana, West Africa, this passage became very real to me. The leaders of our team dropped us off, two by two, in villages to minister for the weekend. They told us they'd come back in a couple days to pick us up. I was a teenager, with another 14-year-old girl, dropped off at a hut without electricity, running water, and no cell phones. Learning my lesson, I would never do that to any teams I have led, but that is what happened to us. On top of that, they asked me to preach the next day—I had never preached a whole sermon before! That night, as I was laying on the dirt floor in a grass hut under my mosquito net, I began to hear bongo drums and the village witch doctor chanting. In that moment I felt very afraid and began to speak Romans 8:15 over myself. I prayed and asked God for protection and the words to speak to the people the next day. When I did that, peace came over my heart. The next day, as I shared the same Scripture that brought me peace the night before, many people got saved, healed, and came to know the love of God.

When you meditate on God's love for you and cast your cares on the Lord, peace comes, faith rises, and fear vanishes. So, what do you do when fear comes? First, guard what you are listening to and watching, and then interrupt the enemy's lies by speaking God's word. What you speak matters. Find promises in His word that relate to the problem you are facing so that you can find the faith to move forward.

For instance, you can speak over your finances through the promise that God will, "supply all my needs according to His riches in glory by Christ Jesus" (Philippians 4:19 NKJV). Or speak over your health with the assurance that you are healed by the stripes of Jesus (1 Peter 2:24). Speak protection over yourself by reciting Psalm 91 and declaring that God is your refuge and fortress, that you trust in Him, and trust that He will command angels to protect you.

In your life, think about what fears you have that may be keeping you stuck or holding you back. Is it fear of failure, fear of safety, or fear of regret? Whatever your fear is, get some of the Scriptures that apply to that area of need and begin to speak them over your life, family, and finances. Put those Scriptures up in your home. Pray and ask God for what you need and then thank Him that He is working in your life. Know that you are loved by your heavenly Father, so choose to move forward in faith.

*Jesus, thank You that Your perfect love casts out fear and right now
I bind the spirit of fear that has tried to grip and control me. I speak
peace to come and flood my home, car, school, and business. Lord, I pray
for divine protection, healing, and miraculous provision. Amen.*

1) What are some things you need to guard in your listening and watching?

_____

_____

_____

2) What are some ways you can interrupt the enemy's lies with God's Word?

_____

_____

_____

3) Share an instance when you experienced fear initially, but God's grace and peace entered the situation.

_____

_____

_____

three

Worry → Worship

Worry is a relative of fear, but it can be more subtle and can weigh us down on a daily basis. These instructions, found in Philippians 4:6-8 (NLT), provide us with guidelines for turning worry into worship:

> *Don't worry about anything; instead, pray about everything. Tell God what you need, and thank him for all he has done. Then you will experience God's peace, which exceeds anything we can understand. His peace will guard your hearts and minds as you live in Christ Jesus. And now, dear brothers and sisters, one final thing. Fix your thoughts on what is true, and honorable, and right, and pure, and lovely, and admirable. Think about things that are excellent and worthy of praise (Philippians 4: 6-8 NLT).*

I once went to a chiropractor to get my neck and back adjusted after traveling, and I couldn't figure out why I was in such pain. He asked me what I was carrying. I said, "Children, laundry, suitcases, you know the normal mom stuff." Then he said to me, "Ok, what do you carry on a daily basis? What is in your purse?" Now he was getting personal.

The chiropractor observed my large purse on the ground, and asked what was in it. I was carrying a "*mother*" purse. My purse was like a Marry Poppins bag; it had everything I might need. When I looked in my bag, I realized I had collected a few water bottles, toys, books, vitamins, old sandwiches, snacks, and all kinds of extra things that were weighing me down. He said something significant to me that day, "I think you need to unload on a daily basis." I needed to take time daily to get rid of unnecessary things so that I wasn't weighed down. I got readjusted, realigned, and began to learn to travel lighter.

Worship brings breakthrough!

We must do the same thing in our journey of faith as followers of God. The Bible shares how, in the book of Matthew, "Jesus said, 'Come to me, all of you who are weary and carry heavy burdens, and I will give you rest. Take my yoke upon you. Let me teach you, because I am humble and gentle at heart, and you will find rest for your souls. For my yoke is easy to bear, and the burden I give you is light'" (Matthew 11:28-30 NLT). When we pray, bringing our cares and worries to God, we are unloading that heavy burden on to God asking Him for help. It's then that we find rest for our souls. To move forward, we must let go of worries that would weigh us down and learn to travel light.

Think about what you are carrying and worrying over every day and consider exchanging those worries for thoughts of gratitude. Thanksgiving, which is worship, is of great importance to this process. When we thank God and when we worship Him, we get our eyes off the problem and on to the promises of God.

In 2 Chronicles 20, there's a powerful story of when the children of Israel were surrounded by enemy armies on all sides and they didn't know what to do. Have you ever felt like that? Have you ever felt surrounded by worry and problems? In this account, the Bible says, King Jehoshaphat feared for a moment then set himself to seek the Lord. As he prayed, he said, "Lord I don't know what to do about this vast army that surrounds me, but my eyes are on You!"

As he sought God, God gave him a strategy. God told him to send the worshippers ahead of his army and assured him that the battle was His to fight. The people of God sang, "give thanks to the Lord for He is good, His love endures forever" (Psalm 136:1 NIV)! Then the Lord sent ambushes against the enemy armies, and they were defeated. The enemies ended up destroying each other. After that, God led them into the Valley of Berakah, which means the valley of blessing. Not only did God deliver them, but they walked into all the prosperity that their enemies had left behind! They ended up better than they started.

Worship brings breakthrough! It is an act of your faith to praise God even when you don't feel like it. And, as you worship, God will begin to give you the wisdom and strategy for your life and your situation.

I've seen this in my own life. When we were living on the mission field in Asia, our son, Isaac, who was three at the time, began to have seizures and stopped breathing on an airplane. We got him breathing again with an oxygen tank and then rushed him to the hospital in Hong Kong as soon as we landed, but the doctors didn't know what to do. He was very weak and continued to have seizures for a month. As I struggled with worry for my son in all the uncertainty, I recall a day that I was sitting with him and the Lord said to me, "sing, Sarah." I knew immediately He wanted me to refocus away from my worry and fear and onto His goodness and provision. Even though I didn't want to do it, I began to give thanks and praise to the Lord. As I worshipped, God brought me supernatural peace and then showed us what to do in the natural and spiritual. After that, he stopped having seizures, regained his strength, and never had another seizure. It was a miracle!

I want to encourage you to exchange worry for worship. Whatever has been weighing you down, take time to pray about it. Like Paul the Apostle shares, "Don't worry about anything; instead, pray about everything. Tell God what you need, and thank him for all he has done. Then you will experience God's peace, which exceeds anything we can understand. His peace will guard your hearts and minds as you live in Christ Jesus" (Philippians 4:6-7 NLT).

Lord, thank You that You see every person, every need, and know every worry. Please bring peace to every storm, and give me wisdom.

Thank You, Lord, that nothing is impossible with You and I trust
You to work in supernatural ways! In Jesus' name, Amen.

1) What cares or worries do you need to bring to God, to talk to Him about, and unload?

_____

_____

_____

2) List some practical ways that you can keep your eyes focused on Jesus when you're surrounded by problems.

_____

_____

_____

3) Share at least five things that you are thankful for. How does our reflection of God's goodness help to alleviate worry?

   1. _____

   2. _____

   3. _____

   4. _____

   5. _____

_____

_____

_____

four

Comparison →»
Unique Purpose

It is easy to look at other people's lives and situations, and subsequently compare your life or yourself with others, especially in the age of social media. Comparison kills joy. It keeps you stuck.

In my own life, I have to guard this on a regular basis, because if I just focus on what everyone else is doing, I won't ever move forward into my unique purpose. 2 Corinthians 10:12 (NIV) reminds us that, "we do not dare to classify or compare ourselves with some who commend themselves. When they measure themselves by themselves and compare themselves with themselves, they are not wise,"

When my kids, Isaac and Lizzy, were much younger, my husband, Caleb, and I took them to an amusement park. I remember when we walked up to one particular ride, there was a measuring stick at the entrance to tell you how tall you had to be in order to ride that ride, but when Lizzy stood up to it, even on her tippy toes, she did not meet the height requirement. She began to cry and said, "Mom, I don't measure up, I don't measure up!" I quickly diverted her attention (as moms do) and said, "It's ok, there are rides made specifically for you, let's go find those!" We did and she soon forgot but I kept thinking of her words, "I don't measure up."

Throw away the measuring stick of comparison and realize you are unique for a purpose!

Lizzy isn't the only one who has been frustrated by comparison. Think about how many times you have pulled out your own measuring stick in your mind and compared yourself with others! Have you ever found these thoughts running through your head? I am too young. I am too old. I am not married. I am married. I have too many kids. I don't have kids. I have a bad past. I have no experience. I'm not good enough. I am not smart enough. I'm not talented enough. I don't have enough money. I don't have the right connections. I don't measure up. I am not enough!

We even compare and measure what God has done in other places or in the past and say, "Well, God can do a thing in that city, but not in my city or in my country." These are lies from the enemy to keep us in a place of mediocrity and fear. We are not to compare ourselves with others or try to limit God in what He can do in and through us. These thoughts of comparison will keep you stuck.

All throughout the Bible, God used ordinary people to do extraordinary things for Him! There was Moses, who didn't think he measured up because of his speech impediment. When God called Moses to deliver the people of Israel out of Egypt, he had all kinds of excuses. He said, "But God who am I? I don't speak eloquently." God said, "I will be with you; I will help you and teach you what to say" (Exodus 3: 11-12). God used Moses to deliver the children of Israel out of slavery and bondage in Egypt!

Gideon didn't think he measured up because he was too weak. When God called Gideon, he was hiding in a cave and said, but Lord, how can I save Israel? My clan is the weakest in Manasseh, and I am the least in my family." The Lord answered, "I will be with you and you will strike down the Midianites together" (Judges 6: 15-16).

Jeremiah didn't think he measured up because he was too young. When God called Jeremiah, he said, "but Lord I don't know how to speak, I am only a youth." The Lord said to him, "Don't say 'I am only a youth.' You must go to everyone I send you to and say whatever I command you. Don't be afraid for I am with you! I will put my words in your mouth" (Jeremiah 1: 6-8). God used Jeremiah as a prophet to speak the word of the Lord to the children of Israel at that time in history.

Sarah didn't think she measured up to God's promise because she was too old. She was, by most measurements, too old to have a child, but had Isaac at 90 years of age. Sarah "considered Him faithful who had made the promise" (Hebrews 11:11 NIV).

Esther didn't think she measured up because she was an orphan and a Jew, but became queen and was used by God to save her people. Mary Magdalene didn't think she measured up because she had a terrible past but she was delivered from demonic spirits, became a follower of Jesus, and was the first to testify of the resurrection of Christ.

Here's the bottom line: God's grace fills in the space where you are lacking— where you don't measure up. Because He is enough, and because He is in you, you have what it takes in Him. Throw away the measuring stick of comparison and realize you are unique for a purpose! God has gifted you for a specific reason. Take an inventory of your gifts, talents, and passions. Then start where you are with what you have. You may think that what you have is not enough, but when you use what you have, God can bless it and multiply it to help others.

*Lord, help me to break free from comparison and walk in the
fullness of the purpose You have for my life. As I start using what
You've given me, please multiply it to bless others. Amen.*

1) What have been some ways that you have felt like you don't measure up?

_____

_____

_____

2) Share an experience of when you stepped forward using your gifts and talents, and found it was enough for the task at hand.

_____

_____

_____

3) We described a lot of people from the Bible who didn't feel like they measured up. Who did you identify most with and why?

_____

_____

_____

five

Perfectionism →» Progress

Comparison and perfectionism can sometimes combine together in a perfect storm that keeps us from progressing to our unique purpose. No one is perfect. We are human. In fact, Jesus was the only perfect person who walked the face of the earth. We are all a work in progress. The Bible says, in Philippians 1:6, that it is God who began this good work in you, and He will be faithful to complete it! God is working in your life to do His good pleasure.

You may not be where you want to be at this moment or season in your life, but you are also not where you used to be. Instead of focusing on things in your life being perfect, focus on progress. Focus on forward movement. Many times, you may feel stuck or as if you are at a standstill, not progressing in your purpose. Despite external factors outside of your control, you can progress in your walk with God and in other areas of your life.

Progress looks different for everyone. For you, progress may be reading this book and growing in faith. Progress may be spending more time reading the Word and in prayer. Forward movement comes in many forms and each step you take increases your stamina to keep going. Celebrate the progress you are making today. Every step of advance is a victory!

When my kids were little and learning to walk, they went through many phases until they achieved that skill. First, they crawled, then pulled up on furniture, and then they were able to stand. After many wobbles and falls they took one step, then two, then three, and then they were off to the races. If they fell down, I didn't get upset. I was just glad they were making progress. I cheered them on and celebrated every step. Your heavenly Father knows exactly where you are, and rejoices over your steps of faith!

We are all in different seasons of life, and advancement comes in many forms. Maybe for those with kids, practical progress is getting through the challenges of schoolwork in an online era. For those with toddlers, how about progress with potty training? Maybe for others, progress is developing a deeper relationship with your older kids. For personal development, forward movement may mean starting an online class to grow in your field of study. Perhaps it may be time to reinvent the way you do work or ministry. Progress could mean getting up and exercising, cleaning your house, or cooking healthy dinners. Whatever dreams are in your heart, take small steps of advancement towards those dreams.

Whatever progress you are making, celebrate it instead of comparing yourself to anyone else. Realize that right now you are planting seeds for a future harvest. A great example is the Chinese bamboo tree. When the bamboo seed is first planted, nothing comes up from the ground for five years. It is watered and fertilized, but there is no visible evidence that anything is happening. Sometime in the fifth year, the bamboo tree will grow up to 90 feet in a six-week span. It can grow three feet in 24 hours! Some people might say, "Wow, that tree just shot up over night!" The truth is that it was growing underground and developing roots. The roots are a precursor to any outward growth.

Progress in our lives is much like the bamboo tree. You may not see overnight results, but as you are preparing and making steps forward, roots are going down deep in you and at the right time you will see a harvest. Galatians 6:9 (NIV) says, "Let us not grow weary while doing good, for in due season we shall reap a harvest if we do not lose heart."

Growing up, I knew I was called into ministry and missions work. As a young person, my dad who was a pastor, encouraged me by saying, "Start here and start now." When I was 17, he asked me to be the kid's pastor for a new service. My dad asked everyone else he could think of who was older and more experienced but they couldn't do it. So, he asked me to oversee it. I was overwhelmed because I didn't know how to lead hundreds of kids. But he believed in me and said I could be creative, so I began to study and research like never before. I built a team of people to help me in various aspects. It wasn't what I was going to do the rest of my life, but it was an assignment for that season! It was challenging, I grew, and I loved it!

After that, God opened the door for me to be a youth pastor for five years, and then young adult pastor for an additional five years. Through that time, we were also leading short term mission trips overseas. When God directed us to move to the mission field to start building children's homes, planting churches, and digging water wells, I realized that He had been preparing me for that moment. As we took steps of faith, God provided each step of the way. Preparation is never lost time! These were dreams I had when I was a little girl but I didn't see them come to pass until later on, after God had prepared me and my roots were deep.

You may not be where you want to be at this moment or season in your life, but you are also not where you used to be.

Martin Luther King, Jr said, "Faith is taking the first step before you see the whole staircase."

What I have learned is that if I wait until everything is perfect, I won't do anything. Planning and preparing are crucial, but sometimes people want to wait until they know everything and have everything figured out before they start moving towards their dream or vision. That only leads to procrastination or inactivity.

The key is progress. Think of the steps you can take towards those dreams. They may seem small, but if you start where you are with what you have, you'll watch God unfold things on your behalf. Sometimes you've got to step out and find out!

> *Lord, help me to choose progress over perfection. Thank You, that You're perfecting all that concerns me and You are faithful to complete the good work You started in me. Help me to nurture the seeds as I am preparing to advance my dreams. Amen.*

1) Can you think of a time(s) when your desire to be perfect has kept you frozen or unable to move forward?

_____

_____

_____

2) Name an occasion in which you started taking steps before you could see where the "staircase" was leading you.

_____

_____

_____

3) What were the results (expected and unexpected) from your willingness to step out in faith?

_____

_____

_____

six

Distractions →» Focus

W e all face distractions. We all have things that need to get done. You may be working, doing homeschool, taking care of the kids, keeping up with laundry, washing dishes, or addressing any other task that needs your attention. Some of the things we have to do are good, but sometimes we can be so distracted that we don't take time to hear God's voice.

Hebrews 12:1-2 (NIV) says, "Therefore, since we are surrounded by such a great cloud of witnesses, let us throw off everything that hinders and the sin that so easily entangles. And let us run with perseverance the race marked out for us, fixing our eyes on Jesus, the pioneer and perfecter of faith. For the joy set before Him He endured the cross, scorning its shame, and sat down at the right hand of the throne of God."

In the middle of all that you have to do and all the chaos around you, focus on what matters. Focus on what God has entrusted to you and what He is speaking to you. God wants to give you clarity in the midst of chaos. He wants to guide you, but we can be so easily weighed down with distractions that we miss it. We must lay aside our distractions and fix our eyes on Jesus.

I remember one particular time I was traveling to go preach in another city. I was alone without kids, so I was enjoying browsing the shops in the airport, reading magazines, and scrolling through social media. I wasn't really paying attention, but I had noticed out of the corner of my eye that my gate was close and boarding, so I got in line to board. After waiting a while in line, when I handed my boarding pass to the gate agent, she looked at me and said, "Girl, are you paying attention? This flight is bound for Jacksonville, Florida and your ticket says Jacksonville, North Carolina! You better run!" I was at the wrong gate. I took off running and realized I had to catch a train go to another terminal to get to my gate, and thankfully I made it. The point is, I was distracted and almost missed getting to my destination!

Have you ever been there? We all get distracted. Life is loud. Our world is loud and there are so many distractions and voices vying for our attention—work, family, friends, music, the TV, our phone notifications, social media, and the list goes on. Some of the voices around us can be good, but some can totally distract us from hearing the voice of God.

Think about what God is speaking to you in this season. Just like the old radios, in which you have to tune past the static to get to the station you want to listen to, we have to do the same thing. We have to tune out all the static and voices of this world that want our attention to tune in to what God is saying. God tells us the Spirit will "guide you into all truth…and he will tell you what is yet to come" (John 16:13 NIV). Take some time to get quiet and hear what God is saying. It doesn't have to take hours — even just a few minutes alone with Him can reveal so much.

God wants to give you clarity in the midst of chaos.

When we look to Jesus and focus on Him, He brings things into perspective. He gives us the right focus for our day, our family, our work, or ministry. In Hebrews 12:2, the Word encourages us that the way we will endure and run our race is by looking to Jesus, the author and finisher of our faith.

Thank you, Lord, that Your Word promises that Your sheep hear Your voice. I choose to lay aside distractions and any hinderances that would keep me from hearing from You and running my race. Help me to focus on You and what You have called me to do in this time and season. Amen.

1) Identify a time when distraction almost put you on a wrong path.

_____

_____

_____

2) What stopped you and helped you to regain focus?

_____

_____

_____

3) What would you consider to be your biggest ongoing distraction and how can you refresh your focus on a daily basis?

_____

_____

_____

seven

Discouragement –» Hope

Discouragement happens! At some point in life, most of us experience discouragement. Things you were expecting to happen didn't happen, or things you had been working towards or planning didn't happen like you thought. My family was planning to be living in Israel for two months in the spring of 2020 because of events my husband was working on, and we were scheduled to be ministering in several countries in Europe as well, but all those plans changed due to the global pandemic. You may be facing major loss or discouragement right now in your life. What we need to remember in the midst of disappointment and discouragement is that we can still move forward in hope.

Whatever you've gone through in the present or past, there is hope.

Hebrews 6:19 (NIV) says, "We have this hope as an anchor for the soul, firm and secure." Jesus is our hope. When we go through challenges, He is the one who can keep us strong. I remember when my dad passed away. He had been the pastor of our home church, Victory, in Tulsa, Oklahoma for 30 years. My husband and I had been living overseas in Asia doing missions work, and we got the call to come home just hours before he passed. We got to see him and talk to him before he went home to be with Jesus, but we still went through major discouragement.

After his memorial service, we were scheduled to be back in Cambodia to do an outreach, women's conference, children's gift giveaway, and finish a church building project. In the natural, I didn't feel I had anything to give. I felt discouraged—like curling up, shutting out the world around me, and giving up.

My mom encouraged me from the example of Jesus in Mark 6, when He found out that his cousin, John the Baptist, had died. Jesus was grieved and went away on a boat to find a solitary place to pray, but when He got to the other side of the lake, He was met with thousands of people waiting to hear what He had to say. In that moment, He saw the multitudes, was moved with compassion, and began to share with them the word of life. Then, when the people needed food, Jesus performed a miracle. A little boy offered Jesus his small lunch of five loaves of bread and two fish, and Jesus took it and blessed it. As the disciples began to hand it out, the food began to multiply and they were able to feed over 5,000 people that day! Not only that but 12 baskets were left over. My mom said, "Sarah, do you realize that Jesus performed a miracle even in the midst of his loss of John the Baptist? I believe if you go to Cambodia and view the people like Jesus, with eyes of compassion, and offer them the hope you have in Christ, He will do miracles beyond what you could imagine! You may feel like what you have is not enough but as you offer it to God, He can multiply it and do the miraculous!"

After she shared that, I knew the Lord was speaking to me through her. As I prayed, God confirmed in my heart that I was to go. The Lord spoke to my heart and reminded me that my dad had run his race with excellence, that I had my own purpose and race to run, and that He had given me grace for my race. We decided to move forward with our travel plans and to continue the work God had called us to despite our discouragement and pain.

As I went, a supernatural joy came in my heart. Joy that was not based on hype but based on hope. When I was there, God reminded me of a vision I had as a little girl of helping orphans and children at risk in other countries. God expanded my vision and I entered a new season of ministry while on that trip that I almost cancelled due to discouragement. He spoke to me about building our first children's home there and began to give me vision to build homes and water wells in other countries. I had no idea how God would provide, but in less than a month, God provided all the funds needed to build that first home. From there, many doors have opened to help children in other countries as well, and now, after 11 years, 27 children's homes and five schools have been built. What God has done is miraculous!

The Lord reminded me of Isaiah 61:3 (NIV) which says that God gives those who grieve a "crown of beauty instead of ashes, the oil of joy instead of mourning, and a garment of praise instead of a spirit of despair." Whatever you've gone through in the present or past, there is hope.

Maybe you've been through a season of loss, but God can give you beauty for ashes and the oil of joy where there has been mourning. Our joy is not based on hype but on our hope in Jesus.

Lord, may hope and joy arise in my heart. I know that no matter what around me is shaken, I have received a Kingdom that cannot be shaken. I put my hope in You and believe that You can work all things together for my good because I love You and am called according to Your purpose. Keep me steady and secure as I anchor my hope in You. Amen.

1) Think of a time when you were overwhelmed with disappointment and/or discouragement, and continued onward in spite of the temptation to quit.

_____

_____

_____

2) Reflect on the time God brought you through disappointment. How did He replace your disappointment?

_____

_____

_____

3) Are there people in your life who would benefit from some encouragement? What hope can you offer to them?

_____

_____

_____

eight

Bitterness —» Forgiveness

In spring time every year, one of my favorite things to do is to plant new flowers in our garden. I start working in my flower bed to clear the ground so that we can plant the fresh flowers. One of the important things you have to do before planting, though, is to pull the weeds that grew during winter so that they don't choke the new plants and seeds being placed in the ground.

We have to do this with our hearts too. Our hearts are like soil and the Word is like a seed. In order for the Word to grow and bear fruit, we have to pull weeds of resentment, bitterness, and offense so they don't choke the good things from growing. Proverbs 4:23 (NIV) says, "above all else, guard your heart, for everything you do flows from it." In the book of Hebrews, the Bible describes bitterness as a root that we must keep from springing up and growing.

In order for us to advance in our walk with God and in the purpose He has for our lives, we have to let go of hurt, bitterness, and offense. It is especially easy during seasons of crisis to get offended. The Bible even says that many will be offended in the last days. Jesus said in Mark 11:25 (NLT), "When you stand praying, first forgive anyone you are holding a grudge against, so that your Father in heaven will forgive your sins, too." Our prayers can be hindered when we choose not to forgive.

Guard your heart. It will be health to your soul and health to your body.

Ephesians 4:32 (NLT) reminds us that we should continually be "forgiving one another, just as God through Christ has forgiven you." You may feel you have the right to hold bitterness, but the price you will pay is not worth it for yourself, your children, or even your health. It only hurts you and it's a burden that the enemy uses to keep you from advancing into all God has for you.

Medical research has been done on the impact of unforgiveness and bitterness. Studies show that holding grudges also affects a person physically. It can cause chemical imbalances, lowers resistance in the immune system, hardens facial features, affects the health of the blood, which can cause bone diseases, and it can cause cancer. Not only is forgiveness good for your soul, it's also good for your body! Bitterness really is like drinking poison and expecting the other person to die.

Forgiveness is not always easy, but it's worth it for your life and for your children, because whatever we carry, we also pass on to our children. Take some time to allow God to search your heart and show you if there is bitterness or offense. Then, ask God for the strength and grace to forgive those who have hurt you. The next step is to reach out to the person who hurt you. The Bible says if your brother has offended you, go to him (Matthew 18). You may need to call that person in a spirit of love and grace. Forgive them and release them. If someone you do not know personally offends you, bless them. Pray for them. The Bible tells us to pray for those who have offended us. Bless those who curse you. They may not reciprocate, but your part of forgiveness will be complete and you can heal.

Forgiveness doesn't excuse their behavior but it prevents it from ruining you. It doesn't mean you go back to that relationship if it was abusive or toxic. You may need to place some boundaries in your life, but you can trust God to be your vindicator. Choose to forgive and bless them. Then speak forgiveness over your emotions so that you stay strong in His grace and don't fall back into bitterness. Forgiveness is like setting a prisoner free only to realize the prisoner was you. Freedom comes when you forgive!

Sometimes after you've forgiven, you won't feel any different. But we don't worship or serve our feelings. You may have to speak to your emotions to get in line with the word of God. Say to yourself, "I am not easily offended! I choose to forgive just as Christ has forgiven me." Don't let bitterness and resentment take root with bosses, spouses, a company, the government, or any entity that presents something offensive to you. Guard your heart. It will be health to your soul and health to your body.

Think about it—how far could you advance if you are UN-offendable? Forgiveness is a choice. Love is a choice.

Father, please give me strength, faith, and grace to forgive and release those who have offended and hurt me. Give me the power and grace to let go and move forward in Your purpose. Help me to guard my heart to avoid offense through Your great love. Amen.

1) Can you think of someone or a situation that you have not forgiven? If so, take a moment to recall and pray a prayer of forgiveness.

_____

_____

_____

2) Think about getting to a point of living where you are virtually UN-offendable. How far could you advance?

_____

_____

_____

3) Are you aware of any situation in which you need to be forgiven? How can you seek reconciliation to assist that person's own health?

_____

_____

_____

nine

Complaining →» Gratitude

Remember the children of Israel who had come out of Egypt, and were headed towards their promised land but they got stuck in the journey? They managed to make an 11-day journey stretch out for 40 years. God spoke to them at the mountain after those 40 years and commanded that they break camp and move forward to the promised land.

Part of their story, found in Numbers 13 and 14, reveals that one of the things that kept them in the wilderness was complaining. They forgot the miracles God had done, how he had parted the Red Sea, rained manna down from heaven, brought water out of a rock, led them by a cloud in the day and fire by night, and continued to complain to God. God was grieved by this and declared that those who complained wouldn't enter the promised land. When we complain, we remain. This is what happened to the complaining children of Israel who had been rescued by God. They stayed stuck in a place of wandering because of complaining and unbelief.

The Bible is very clear that we are to choose gratitude in all circumstances. Break free from complaining and move forward with gratitude. 1 Thessalonians 5:18 (NKJV) says, "In everything give thanks; for this is the will of God in Christ

Jesus for you." All throughout the Bible, God directs us to give thanks. There are 116 references to thanksgiving and we are told to give thanks directly 73 times! This verse lets us know that it is God's will for us to give thanks. That doesn't mean that we thank God for the problems we have, but we can still find something to be grateful for in every situation or challenge. Right now, in our world, everything seems to be constantly shifting and it's easy to complain, but we can always find things to be grateful for.

When we complain, we remain.

I recently went out for a bike ride with my family, and I noticed one of my kids kept looking back and drifting off course. I encouraged him to look ahead so he could stay on course and not veer off. I thought about how, for each person, it's natural for us to drift like that, looking back and thinking negatively. The spirit of negativity can cause you to drift so far off course that you miss the destiny God has for your life. That's why we have to make a conscious effort to focus on gratitude.

There are many obstacles to gratitude, but here are seven that we must over-come to allow a spirit of gratitude to take over.

1) Excessive noise
2) Over exposure to media
3) Attitude of entitlement
4) Worry or negative forecasting
5) Materialism and consumerism
6) Scarcity mentality
7) Lack of connection and intimacy with God

When you connect with God, you naturally and humbly cherish life for what it is—a temporary gift. Gratitude is a choice we make. Joyce Meyer says it best: "Complain and remain or praise and be raised."

Gratitude attracts the favor and blessing of God! It is an acknowledgment that everything you have comes from God. Gratitude allows you to shine brighter in this dark world. We are told, "Do everything without grumbling or arguing, so that you may become blameless and pure, 'children of God without fault in a warped and crooked generation.' Then you will shine among them like stars in the sky as you hold firmly to the word of life" (Philippians 2:14-16 NIV).

Right now, think of things you are grateful for. Write down a list of ten things you can be grateful for—even talk about it with your kids and spouse. It could save your marriage. It can bring joy and lighten the mood. Let's break free from complaining and move forward with gratitude!

Lord, empower me to choose to break free from complaining and choose gratitude. I thank You God for life, breath, and all You've given me. Amen.

1) List any other obstacles you may have experienced that hinder gratitude.

_____

_____

_____

2) List 10 things for which you are grateful.

1. _____

_____

2. _____

_____

3. _____

_____

4. _____

_____

5. _____

_____

6. _____

7. _____

8. _____

9. _____

10._____

3) Share your "gratitude" list with those closest to you.

ten

Scarcity –» Generosity

Proverbs 11:24 (MSG) says, "The world of the generous gets larger and larger; the world of the stingy gets smaller and smaller." In our world, there is a lot of fear—fear of lack and fear of the future, but God doesn't want us to live with a scarcity mindset. You may feel as if what you have is not enough, personally, or in regard to the dreams God has put in your heart. What you can do is think about what is in your hand. Even if what you have in your hand is not enough to accomplish your dream, maybe what you have is a seed.

When we sow a seed in faith, God can multiply it!

There's a story in Mark 6 when Jesus was teaching a group of people and a crowd of over 5,000 men had gathered to hear from Him, and as it got late in the day, they became hungry. They were far from any food, so Jesus told the disciples to find something for them to eat. The only thing they could find was a little boy with a lunch of five loaves and two fish. That little boy offered what was in his hand to Jesus, and Jesus blessed it and it multiplied to feed over 5,000 people! They even had 12 baskets left over. A miracle happened in the midst of a situation where there seemed to be lack.

There have been times in my life when I felt that what was in my hand was not enough. I remember when I was in Cambodia for the first time in 2009, we were hosting a Christmas outreach, and I walked into the church to get the food we were going to distribute. When I walked in, there were children that had been sleeping on the floor of the church who were dirty and barely clothed, and they began to scatter in fear. I asked the pastor who the children were and he said most were abandoned and were at risk of being trafficked, so they let them sleep on the floor of the church. I was shocked and knew we had to do something, but I wasn't sure what or how.

We were living as missionaries in Hong Kong at the time, and after we went back home to Hong Kong, I couldn't forget those children. I felt the Lord challenging me that we were to build a home for them and help them, but we didn't have the money to do that. I went to my husband and he said, "I think that's great, but I'm believing for the miracle each month just to live on the mission field, so you are going to have to believe God for that because I'm believing for a lot as it is."

I didn't know how to start but I felt God ask me, "What's in your hand?" I had a little seed offering to give and I had faith that God could do it. That weekend, I was hosting a women's conference in Hong Kong with our church there and I thought–I have an opportunity in my hand. I shared it first with the pastor to get his opinion, and he said, "Yes let's do it!" I shared the vision with the women—and within ten days, God supernaturally provided all the funds to build that first children's home in Cambodia. It was finished in 2010 and, since then, God has provided resources to build over 27 other homes in other Southeast Asian nations like Burma, Thailand, and Nepal. It was like God multiplying the little boy's lunch. It was, and has continued to be, a miracle!

The other thing that I realized is that there are always people on the other side of your obedience to God. There are recipients to your obedience, as well as those who need to join you in your obedience. Sometimes we feel like what we have is not enough for ourselves or for the vision God has given us, but God can make much out of little when we ask. When we sow a seed in faith, God can multiply it!

The Bible says in Genesis 8:22 (NLT), "As long as the earth remains there will be planting and harvest." It also says in Luke 6:38 (NIV), "Give, and it will be given to you. A good measure, pressed down, shaken together and running over, will be poured into your lap. For with the measure you use, it will be measured to you." God is more than enough. He is called Jehovah Jireh, which means our provider. Put your trust in the Lord today. Maybe you are believing for a job, or provision in some area. The first thing you can do is pray. Ask God for it. Then think of a seed you can sow in faith believing that God will multiply it for a harvest.

We all have a seed to sow. It may not seem like much, but it has the power to multiply. If you need hope, give some hope away. If you need more time, give God the first part of your day. If you need help, pray for someone else. If your finances are lacking, sow a financial seed. This principle works in every nation. There is someone you can have an impact on! There's always someone on the other side of your obedience.

Lord, I believe You for provision. I pray as I sow seeds, that You would multiply them and bring a harvest into my life in supernatural ways! God, You are no respecter of persons. Your Word works in every nation, every culture, and nothing is too hard for You. Amen.

1) Think of a time you have had little but God multiplied what you had to meet the need you were experiencing.

_____

_____

_____

2) Who was on the other side of your obedience?

_____

_____

_____

3) What dream is in your heart now? What do you have in your hand to begin
the process?

_____

_____

_____

eleven

Panic →» Peace

It is easy for our minds to slip into feelings of panic and fear. Thankfully, we are assured in Isaiah 26:3-4 (NIV) that, "you will keep in perfect peace those whose minds are steadfast, because they trust in you. Trust in the LORD forever, for the LORD, the LORD himself, is the Rock eternal." With God's help, you can exchange thoughts of panic for the peace of God!

Have you ever bought an item at a store or ordered something online, but then when you got it home, it didn't fit like you expected or work like you thought? This happens to me sometimes, but the good thing is that I don't have to keep it. I am able to send it back and make an exchange for something that fits and works for me.

The Lord wants to deliver you from the spirit of fear and panic.

We must do the same thing when it comes to our thought life and our words. When the enemy starts to attack us with lies of fear or panic, we have a choice to make. We have the choice to exchange thoughts of fear for faith, thoughts of panic for peace, and anxiety for trust. We exchange negative thoughts with the Word of God and let His peace guard our hearts and minds. 2 Corinthians 10:5 reminds us that we can take our thoughts captive and make them obedient to Christ.

How? By renewing our minds with the Word of God. Ephesians 4:23 (AMPC) is clear in instructing us "to be constantly renewed in the spirit of your mind [having a fresh mental and spiritual attitude]." This is not a one and done thing. This is constant, continual renewal on a daily basis. God's Word works to renovate our minds. Think of your favorite home renovation show and how you see a transformation take place from start to finish. God's Word renovates our minds! It renews our souls. If you are struggling with thoughts of panic or fear, seek the ultimate renovation expert to renew your thoughts— God! Through His Word and guidance from the Holy Spirit, you can defeat those thoughts.

After my dad passed away, I started dealing with fear and anxiety. It was affecting my health, and after praying about it, I realized I was doubting God's goodness towards me. I was doubting that God would take care of me. I had to renew my mind with the Word and take authority over my thoughts. I had to feed on His faithfulness before my mind shifted away from that negative mindset. Psalm 37:3 (NKJV) tells us to "trust in the Lord, and do good; dwell in the land, and feed on His faithfulness." Analyze what you're feeding to your Spirit. What are you feeding your mind? We must intentionally focus on feeding on His faithfulness. One of the ways you can do that is to get a couple Scriptures, meditate on them daily, and then speak them out loud.

A great place to start is with Psalm 34:4 (NIV), which is a truth you can stand on: "I sought the Lord and he answered me; he delivered me from all my fears." The Lord wants to deliver you from the spirit of fear and panic. It doesn't have to control you. You can have peace in your mind.

God, please fill me with Your perfect peace. Help me to immerse myself in Your Word to remind myself of Your faithfulness and Your promises so that I can guard my heart and mind. Amen.

1) Can you identify any negative thoughts or feelings you are currently having?

_____

_____

_____

2) Exchange that thought now with Scripture. Write down that thought in one column and the Scripture in the other. Determine to make that transition.

_____

_____

_____

twelve

Defeat →» Victory

L ooking back at the rescued children of Israel, Numbers 13 tells of when Moses sent twelve spies to check out the promised land. Ten came back with a negative report. They said that there were giants in the land and that they looked like grasshoppers. They were defeated by how they saw themselves and spoke defeat which kept them stuck in the wilderness. They had a mindset and a language of defeat.

Two other spies, Joshua and Caleb, had a different spirit. Joshua came back and said, "The land, which we passed through to spy it out, is an exceedingly good land. If the Lord delights in us, He will bring us into this land and give it to us, a land that flows with milk and honey" (Number 14:7-8 ESV). They saw the same giants that the other spies did but they focused instead on how great their God was and spoke victory even before they saw it!

This one thing set them apart. Sadly, none of the ten spies who doubted that God could help them go in and possess the promised land went in. Joshua and Caleb went in with faith that God could help them and bring them the victory. In the midst of crisis, and in the midst of giants of fear, one of the greatest ways we move forward is in the words that we speak. Are you speaking a "language of defeat" or are you speaking a "language of victory?" You can declare your faith in God through what He has already provided for you. Anyone can align their words with their circumstances, but as people of faith, we are called to align our words with how great our God is and what His word says. Speak His promises over your life.

By faith, we receive all the promises of God, not just for salvation, but healing, provision, peace, joy, or whatever your promise is. Faith is not just believing but speaking. In 2 Corinthians 4:13 it says, the spirit of faith is: I believe and therefore I speak. This does not mean we deny reality. What is does indicate is that we should emphasize our belief in His word above our circumstances.

Jonathan, a young man in our church, was diagnosed with cancer in his knee when he was 16 years old. He was a track star and had been offered a college scholarship. But the doctors said the cancer was so bad that they were going to have to amputate his knee. He and his family made a decision not to tell people the negative report, but instead they took two weeks to focus on prayer and speak the word of faith over his body. In fact, they began to call him *Jonathan New Knees.*

They filled their home with an environment of faith by playing healing scripture CD's and songs. They called me over, since I was one of Jonathan's youth pastors at the time, to pray for him, but before I even got there, they made a decision to believe God for a miracle. After two weeks, they went to the doctor and he couldn't find the cancer. Jonathan was totally healed!

Sometimes we worry about things and don't move forward because we are not asking God. During this past year, the Lord dealt with me to begin prophesying over areas I was wanting to see change in and that I needed to speak faith over things that seemed to be hopeless.

By faith, we receive all the promises of God, not just for salvation, but healing, provision, peace, and joy.

There is a story in Ezekiel 37, when God showed Ezekiel a vision of a valley of dry, dead bones. God told him to prophecy over those dry bones, and he spoke to them. As he spoke life, the bones began to rattle, form flesh, breathe, and came together to form an army! Ezekiel's words signified restoration for the Israelites and demonstrated God's power to work through those words.

My encouragement to you today is to prophecy over the dry or dead dreams in your life. Death and life are in the power of the tongue. James 3 points out that our tongue is like the rudder on a ship, or a bit in a horse's mouth. It's small, but it can direct the whole body. Speak life over all aspects of your life. Every day when I get up and spend time with God, I declare His promises over my life, health, family, marriage, children, and finances. I go out and walk outside and have a list of Scriptures that I declare every day over my children, over my mind, over my heart, and my body. As we renew our minds with God's Word, we allow His spirit to transform our thinking, our speaking, and it transforms the way we live. Speaking His promises will produce faith that grows confidence in our lives.

Speak life, faith, and blessing! Then, you'll find greater boldness to take the steps you need to take. You are called to live a life of victory and advance in every area.

Lord, I thank You that Your resurrection power lives in me, and that I can walk in the victory that You have already given me because of Jesus! Help me to speak Your promises over my life. Let Your kingdom come, and Your will be done in me and through me as it is in heaven. Amen.

1) What challenging circumstances are you facing now that require you to align your words with the Word of God?

_____

_____

_____

2) What Scriptures do you know that can address your current challenges?

_____

_____

_____

3) Share an experience in which you spoke life into a situation and God worked through your words to bring victory.

_____

_____

_____

thirteen

Surviving →» Thriving

You were made not just to survive, but to thrive and be fruitful. That doesn't mean that you won't face storms or challenges in this life, but it does mean that in the midst of the challenges, you can still thrive. You were made to flourish!

When my husband, Caleb, and I were living in Orlando, Florida, there was a major hurricane in the fall of 2016 that affected a lot of that area and surrounding coastal areas. Before that big hurricane, the news organizations encouraged people to board up their houses and prepare for this big storm. So, we were prepared and were praying it would pass over. I remember during the storm looking out the window at our palm trees in the front yard. They were being pushed down all the way to the ground and all around. I kept thinking they would snap in two, but they didn't. They just bounced right back up after the storm! Afterwards, I was studying the palm tree, and I learned that the date palm tree is so resilient that, during a storm, the more it's pressed down the more it grows, and the more its root system is strengthened! It has strong roots, has the incredible ability to bounce back after a storm, is abundantly fruitful and fragrant, nothing is wasted (every part of it is useful), and it represented praise and a symbol of victory in the bible.

In this life, we will all face pressure, storms, and trials (in the natural and in the spiritual realm). In fact, Jesus said in John 16:33 (NKJV), "In this world you will have tribulation, but be of good cheer because I have overcome the world!" You may be facing storms and pressure during this season in your finances, career, marriage or family, and health. Whatever type of storm or pressure it is, we know it's the devil that comes to steal, kill and destroy, but Jesus has given us everything we need to overcome, walk in victory, and flourish.

Just like the palm tree, you have the ability to "bounce back" on the inside and flourish, because the same spirit that raised Christ lives in you! Psalm 92:12-15 (AMP) says:

> *The righteous will flourish like the date palm [long-lived, upright and useful]; They will grow like a cedar in Lebanon [majestic and stable]. Planted in the house of the LORD, they will flourish in the courts of our God. [Growing in grace] they will still thrive and bear fruit and prosper in old age; They will flourish and be vital and fresh [rich in trust and love and contentment]; [They are living memorials] to declare that the LORD is upright and faithful [to His promises]; He is my rock, and There is no evil in Him!*

This is what we are called to do, no matter what the enemy tries to bring against us. We keep on bouncing back like the palm tree; we stay strong, remain fruitful, and a testimony of God's faithfulness!

I am reminded of the story of Jesus and his disciples when they faced a storm in Mark 4:35-41 (ESV):

> *"On that day, when evening had come, he said to them, 'Let us go across to the other side.' And leaving the crowd, they took him with them in the boat, just as he was. And other boats were with him. And a great windstorm arose, and the waves were breaking into the boat, so that the boat was already filling. But he was in the stern, asleep on the cushion. And they woke him and said to him, 'Teacher, do you not care that we are perishing?' And he awoke and rebuked the wind and said to the sea, 'Peace! Be still!'*

And the wind ceased, and there was a great calm. He said to them, 'Why are you so afraid? Have you still no faith?' And they were filled with great fear and said to one another, 'Who then is this, that even the wind and the sea obey him?'"

There are three keys from this passage that can help you overcome in the midst of the storms of life. The first is to remember that Jesus is with you! In this passage when the storm arose, the disciples were afraid and began to yell at Jesus, "Don't you care that we are going to die?!" They were focused on the waves and forgot who was in their boat. They forgot that the Creator of the universe, the King of kings, and Lord of Lords was with them! Sometimes we can get so focused on the circumstances we can forget who is in our boat. Remember, Jesus is with you!

Several years ago, I was driving in Tulsa while it was raining and got a flat tire. I pulled over and realized I didn't have a spare. I called to try to hire someone to come help me, but they couldn't arrive until two hours later. So, I was stranded on the side of the road in the pouring rain until they could come, and it was going to cost me more than I wanted. After the whole ordeal, I was telling my mom about it and she said, "Don't you remember that I bought you a membership to AAA for Christmas and you have access to roadside assistance for free? And they will come right away!" I said, "What?! I don't remember that." I didn't realize or remember what I already had access to.

On the other side of our storms or struggles there are people God has called us to reach!

Sometimes, as believers, we can forget what we have access to through Christ. We have to get our Bible out and read our inheritance in Christ. We need to be rooted in the Word, so we are not stranded without hope in the midst of the storm. On a daily basis, we need to refuel with the Word of God, prayer, and remind ourselves of God's goodness and faithfulness.

The second thing to remember is to speak peace. In the middle of the storm, Jesus stood up and spoke to the waves, "Peace! Be still!" And the waves stopped. The disciples were focused on talking about how big the waves were, but Jesus was focused on speaking peace to the storm. Jesus has given us authority over the enemy, and we take authority with the words we speak. Our words are powerful, and have the power of life or death. Words of faith can change a situation.

I remember sharing principles like this when we were living in Hong Kong as missionaries. I was preaching at the church we were a part of there, and after my sermon, a lady came up to me afterwards and shared how she couldn't sleep at night. She was having nightmares and fear was tormenting her. After talking to her a while, I realized she still believed in ancestor worship (talking to relatives who had passed on) and I told her that was an open door to the enemy. She renounced those things and asked Jesus to come into her heart. Then I told her to go home and pray over her home and speak the passage in Psalm 127:2 that says, "He gives his beloved sweet sleep." The next week she came back and looked like a new person. She was rested and happy. She came up to me and said, "It works! The Word works! I've been able to sleep now and haven't had any more nightmares. The word works! It is alive and powerful!"

The third key to remember is that people are waiting for you! Right after the disciples got through the storm and made it to the other side in Matthew 5:1-20, there was a demon possessed man who had been living in the tombs who came out crying for help. When he saw Jesus, he fell to his knees and screamed. Jesus commanded the spirits to come out of him and sent the demons into a herd of pigs. When the local people saw what happened, they were in awe. The man wanted to go with Jesus, but He said no, and directed him to go back to his city and tell them what the Lord had done. So, the man when away and began to share in the Decapolis what Jesus had done for him. On the other side of the storm was a man who needed freedom and a city that needed Jesus! What we must realize, is that on the other side of our storms or struggles there are people God has called us to reach!

Caleb and I were praying when our world went through a global pandemic and everything shut down. God put it on our hearts to start food outreaches in Cambodia in the villages. We've been working in that country with pastors for over ten years, so we knew it was possible to reach new, rural villages with the gospel, but we didn't have the provision at first. As we started with one month reaching into ten villages, God brought the increase. Within nine months, 81 villages and counting, were reached with food and the gospel, and we are continuing to reach more. You never know who is on the other side of your storm. Don't give up.

Remember these keys: Jesus is with you, speak peace to the storm, and people are waiting for you! Be encouraged today knowing that God is with you, He is for you and He will give you the grace to overcome whatever storm you may face!

Lord, I thank You that Your Word remains true through every storm and trial that I face. Thank You for the peace to prevail, and the opportunity to bless someone on the other side of my trouble. Amen.

1) Share an experience in which another person trusted Jesus in their storm and you were the person on the other end who received help.

_____

_____

_____

2) Share an experience in which you were able to prevail with Jesus through a troubling time and who you were able to help.

_____

_____

_____

fourteen

Confusion —» Clarity

God wants to give you clarity in the midst of chaos. With all the voices in the world vying for our attention daily, it is so important that we hear God's voice and get His direction for our life. Jesus said in John 10:27 (NKJV), "My sheep hear my voice, and I know them, and they follow Me."

Some people think hearing from God is just for pastors or preachers but this promise tells us that we can all hear God's voice. You have direct access to God's voice. This is why Jesus gave us the Holy Spirit—to live in us, lead us, and guide us. John 16:13 promises that the Spirit will guide you and show you things to come. Hearing from God is one of the most important things we can focus energy on because He created you and His plans for you are good! Clarity comes when you ask God for wisdom and then take the time to hear what He is saying.

There's an old story about a farmer who went to visit his friend in New York City. They were walking through Times Square in the middle of New York during lunch hour. The streets were filled with people. Cars were honking their horns, taxicabs were squealing around corners, sirens were wailing, and the sounds of the city were almost deafening. Suddenly, the farmer said, "I hear a cricket."

His friend said, "What? You must be crazy. You couldn't possibly hear a cricket in all this noise!"

"No, I'm sure of it," the farmer said, "I hear a cricket."

"That's crazy," his friend insisted.

The farmer listened carefully for a moment and then walked across the street to a big cement planter filled with shrubs. He looked under the branches and, sure enough, he found a small cricket. His friend was utterly amazed.

"That's incredible," his friend said. "You must have superhuman ears!"

"No," the farmer said. "My ears are no different from yours. This is just what I'm tuned into. It all depends on what you're listening for."

"But that can't be!" said the friend. "I could never hear a cricket in this noise."

"Yes, that's true," came the reply. "It depends on what is really important to you. Here, let me show you."

He reached into his pocket, pulled out a handful of coins, and discreetly dropped them on the sidewalk. Then, with the noise of the crowded street still blaring in their ears, they noticed every head within twenty feet turn and look to see if the money that had tinkled on the pavement was theirs.

"See what I mean?" asked the Farmer. "It all depends on what's important to you."

This story highlights an important thought. What are you tuned into? Are you listening to the heart of God, His voice, or what the world is saying? Take time to get quiet and tune out distractions to hear what He is saying.

Maybe you are trying to discern the next step you should take. The Bible says in James 1:5-8 (NIV), "If any of you lacks wisdom, you should ask God, who gives generously to all without finding fault, and it will be given to you. But when you ask, you must believe and not doubt, because the one who doubts is like a wave of the sea, blown and tossed by the wind. That person should not expect to receive anything from the Lord. Such a person is double-minded and unstable in all they do."

Clarity comes when you ask God for wisdom and then take the time to hear what He is saying.

If you are needing clarity in decisions you need to make, the first thing to do is to ask God. Have confidence that you do hear God's voice because you are His child, and He will show you the steps to take. He will give you the direction that you need. It may not be what you thought it was going to be, but if you listen and are obedient, you will see His good plan worked out in your life. He may speak to you through His Word, through a Scripture, through a message you hear, or through the still small voice of the Holy Spirit. However He chooses to speak to you, it will always line up with the truth of Scripture.

Lord, I pray for clarity in the midst of chaos. Show me the steps I need to take, and fill me with Your peace. I commit to tuning in to Your voice and look with anticipation for the wisdom that You will share with me. Amen.

1) Can you identify an area in your life right now that seems unclear and/ or chaotic?

_____

_____

2) Ask God now for wisdom in this particular area and then listen for His voice and follow His guidance.

_____

_____

3) Search the Word of God for alignment with what you are hearing from Him.

_____

_____

_____

fifteen

Weariness →» Strength

We all go through times when we feel weary. Sometimes, we can get weary trying to figure everything out, but the Bible says in Isaiah 40:31 (NASB), "Those who wait for the LORD [who expect, look for, and hope in Him] will gain new strength *and* renew their power; they will mount up with wings [and rise up close to God] like eagles [rising toward the sun]; They will run and not get tired, they will walk and not become weary."

The translation of this word "wait" in this Scripture means those that expect, look for, and hope in Him will renew their strength. The usage of the word "wait" is not a passive word. This is active. When you feel weary and tired, the act of putting your hope and trust in the Lord will cause you to be renewed with strength. Just as our bodies need fuel and our cars need gas, our spirit needs the presence of God. As we wait on Him, He replenishes us.

The other way we stand strong in the Lord is by putting on the armor of God. Ephesians 6:10-11, 17 (NLT) tells us to, "Be strong in the Lord and in His mighty power. Put on all of God's armor so that you will be able to stand firm against all strategies of the devil ... and take the sword of the Spirit, which is the Word of God." These are both ways to strengthen yourself.

When Caleb and I first moved to Hong Kong, I decided to go out for a run around our apartment complex. As I was running, I turned a corner to find something I'd only seen in movies. Right in front of me was a Chinese woman with a huge Samurai sword pointing right at me! Immediately, I imagined the music in the background, *Everybody Was Kung Fu Fighting*.

As I stopped and looked around, I realized there wasn't just one woman— there was a whole group of them. They were on guard with their swords drawn, practicing a form of Chinese martial arts. Their eyes were serious, fixed and determined, and they were not about to move out of the way for me. As quickly as I could, I turned right around and ran in the other direction. That was my initiation to Asia.

Just as our bodies need fuel and our cars need gas, our spirit needs the presence of God.

Later, I thought back on that story and recognized its relevance to our lives as believers. It is incredibly crucial for us to be aware that in this race of life we're running, the enemy will try to stop us. He will try to hold us back from fulfilling our destiny. He wants us to give up. He wants us to see roadblocks and turn the other way. He will use what he can: lies of fear, failure, or anxiety. That's why we must put on our armor of strength and take up the sword of the Spirit, which is the spoken Word of God, against the lies of the enemy. When you speak the Word of God, you are pulling out a sword and moving forward in your race.

Lord, I pray for strength to rise up in me as I speak Your Word over my life and my race. I have a purpose and a calling, and I will not allow the lies of the enemy to stop me from running. As I wait on You, I thank You that You are renewing my strength. In Jesus' name, Amen.

1) What are some road blocks you have ran into in your spiritual race? Are any of them recurring?

_____

_____

_____

2) Based on this passage in Ephesians, what does it mean to "take up your sword" against the enemy?

_____

_____

_____

3) Write down some scriptures that apply to the situations you are facing right now that you can speak over your life.

_____

_____

_____

sixteen

Heaviness →» Joy

Why do we need joy? The Bible says, "The joy of the Lord is your strength" (Nehemiah 8:10 NIV). We need strength to fulfill our purpose. Your heart may feel heavy because you are trying to figure out the future and you're worried about uncertainty. We have all been there. You need to know, though, that God wants to give you joy in the journey! We can choose to rejoice. Isaiah 61:3 (NKJV) says, "Put on the garment of praise for the spirit of heaviness." When we praise God, we don't rejoice because of any outward circumstances or hype. Our joy is based on our hope in Jesus.

I remember one night several years ago I was driving to the airport with my kids to go pick up my husband, Caleb, from the airport. It was late and my kids were young at the time. Caleb was coming back from a mission trip, and my son, Isaac, who was five at the time, noticed we were on a road to the airport that was different than usual. He is very inquisitive and has a great memory for directions and he began to ask me 20 questions impatiently.

"Mom, where are we going? Mom, are you sure this is the right way? This doesn't look like the normal way! Is Daddy going to be there? Is he going to bring me a present? How long is it going to take us? Mom... are we there yet?!" And on and on he went.

I calmed him down, and said, "It's okay Isaac, Mommy knows where she is going. We will get there on time. Daddy will be there, and if he said he will bring you a present, he will. Just be patient, trust me, and enjoy the journey!"

After that conversation, I felt the Holy Spirit nudge my heart and remind me too of the same lesson, "Sarah, I am saying the same thing to you. Trust me, follow my lead and enjoy where you are on the way to where you are going!"

You may very well be in a season of waiting right now. Waiting for an answer to prayer, waiting for a dream to come to pass, or waiting for something to change, and I want to encourage you to trust in the Lord. He is with you. Even in the waiting time of life, take time to praise God. He is for you and He can give you joy in every season when you choose to rejoice.

The Apostle Paul was thrown into prison for preaching the Gospel. He wasn't expecting to be in that situation, but in the midst of it, he chose to make the most of it and write the epistles to the church of Philippi. In Philippians 4:4, 11, and 13 (NIV) he says, "Rejoice in the Lord always. I will say it again: Rejoice... I have learned to be content regardless of my circumstance... I can do all things through Christ who gives me strength." Paul gives us a great example of keeping joy on the journey no matter what the circumstances may be. He chose to rejoice and be content because he knew God was with him.

In fact, in Acts 16, when he and Silas were thrown into jail, he began to sing and praise God at midnight. I've been in the underground jail in Rome where the Apostle Paul was, and it is dark, damp, and dirty. Even in his lockdown, he began to praise God. As he began to praise, God sent an earthquake! The jail began to shake, the doors flew open, and their chains fell off. All the prisoners were freed, and the jailer was so worried about his own fate, he was going to kill himself. But Paul stopped him and led that jailer, and then his family, to Jesus! God used a moment when they were in lockdown to send revival to that jail because Paul and Silas chose to rejoice. God brought breakthrough not only to Paul, but also to the jailer, because of Paul's choice to rejoice.

Having joy on the journey doesn't mean we don't face challenges, but it means we can rejoice because we know that we have the greater One living in us that helps us to overcome! When you choose to rejoice through all circumstances, you experience breakthrough.

Our joy is not based on hype but on our hope in Jesus!

Through our joy, we receive strength to carry out God's will in our life. In John 16:33 (NKJV) Jesus said, "In this world you will have tribulation, but be of good cheer (rejoice), for I have overcome the world!'" Joy is an outward sign of our inward faith in the promises of God!

Lord, as I choose to rejoice despite my circumstances, I trust that I will be filled with Your joy and peace! I pray for the strength to carry out Your purpose in my life. Help me to trust You, and enjoy the journey You have designed for me. Amen.

1) Describe a time you have completed and "assignment" from God in the midst of challenging circumstances.

_____

_____

_____

2) Describe a time in which you experienced the "joy" of the Lord during a difficult time.

_____

_____

_____

3) What would you need to change in order to have consistent joy as you fulfill
   your purpose?

_____

_____

_____

seventeen

Selfishness →» Compassion

One of the ways that you can continue to advance is to show compassion to others. Compassion is love in action! Galatians 5:13 (NLT) reminds us, "for you have been called to live in freedom, my brothers and sisters. But don't use your freedom to satisfy your sinful nature. Instead, use your freedom to serve one another in love." God has called us to be rivers of His love, not reservoirs.

This principle was illustrated to me when I visited Israel, and saw The Sea of Galilee and the Dead Sea. The Sea of Galilee is Israel's largest freshwater lake and is fed by the Jordan River, which flows through it from north to south. Water flows in and out of that lake. There is a constant flow. Galilee's shore has rich soil, which enables plants to flourish, and many types of fish live in the Sea of Galilee, providing fisherman with great sustenance.

On the other hand, nothing lives in the Dead Sea. There are no plants or seaweed of any kind around the water. The Dead Sea is continually fed water from rivers and streams coming off the mountains that surround it, but no rivers drain out of it. There is no outlet. As a result, it has become stagnate, and nothing is able to live in it.

These polar opposite bodies of water show us a picture of how our lives can become. We can receive and share, or we can receive and hold on to what we get. We can receive a lot of head knowledge from the Bible, but if we don't give out of ourselves on a regular basis, we become stagnant. God has called us not only to receive from His Word on a daily basis, but also to give out His love and message of hope to others. Matthew 10:8 (NIV) says, "Freely you have received; freely give." You are called to be an ambassador of God and His love to the world. You are anointed to bring hope to the people around you.

Right now, people are more open than ever to receive the hope you have in Jesus. There are people in your sphere of influence who need you to share God's love and hope with them. It could mean calling someone you know to check on them, texting someone that you are praying for them, or blessing someone in need. We may not be able to do everything, but we can do something.

My grandma shared with me that after her husband, my grandpa, passed away, she was very lonely and discouraged. She was in her rocking chair for weeks until my dad came by and encouraged her to look for ways to help others. As she did, love started growing—now, at 96 years old, she is still calling people, encouraging, and blessing others.

Each one of us can do something. Don't get overwhelmed by the big needs out there. Just do something with what you have. I encourage you to think of some way you can be an outlet of the love of God. Be a river of compassion, not a reservoir of stagnation. Think of someone you can bless or someone you can encourage. It's amazing the joy it brings to your own heart when you begin to flow in God's compassion. He will always refill you.

Dear Lord, today I move forward in love. Give me Your heart for people and help me to be moved with compassion towards them. Make me a river of Your love! Amen.

1) Why do you think it may be difficult at times to share what we know about God's love with others?

_____

_____

_____

2) Share a story of how another person was compassionate towards you and shared God's love freely.

_____

_____

_____

3) What are some practical ways you can share God's love with someone today?

_____

_____

_____

eighteen

Lack ➜ Provision

Another way we move forward in our purpose is to realize the access we have to all God's promises. Ephesians 2:18 (NKJV) says, "For through Him, we both have access by one Spirit to the Father." The Bible is full of promises that we have access to as followers of Jesus Christ.

There is a story of a man who wanted to travel to the United States from Europe. This was before traveling by plane was common, and most people traveled by boat. The man worked hard, saved as much as he could, and finally had just enough money to purchase a ticket aboard a cruise ship. At that time, these ships required about two to three weeks to cross the ocean. He went out and bought a suitcase and filled it full of cheese and crackers. That's all he could afford.

Once aboard, all the other passengers went to the large, ornate dining room to eat their gourmet meals. Meanwhile, the poor man would go over in the corner and eat his cheese and crackers. This went on day after day. He could smell the delicious food being served in the dining room. He heard the other passengers speak of it in glowing terms as they rubbed their bellies and complained how full they were. The poor man wanted to join the other guest in the dining room, but he had no extra money.

Toward the end of the trip, another man came up to him and said, "Sir, I can't help but notice that you are always over there eating those cheese and crackers at mealtimes. Why don't you come into the banquet hall and eat with us?"

The traveler's face flushed with embarrassment, "well, to tell you the truth, I had only enough money to buy the ticket. I don't have any extra money to purchase fancy meals." The other passenger raised his eyebrows in surprise. He shook his head and said, "Sir, don't you realize the meals are included in the price of the ticket? Your meals have already been paid for!"

Many people are like the naïve traveler; they are saved and have their "ticket" to heaven, but they don't realize all that God has provided for them here on earth. God has set a banquet table of provision for you in His Word! Second Peter 1:3 (NLT) says, "By His divine power, God has given us everything we need for living a godly life. We have received all of this by coming to know him, the one who called us to himself by means of his marvelous glory and excellence."

Anytime we walk around in fear or say, "I can't do that; I don't have what it takes," we are eating more cheese and crackers. Some have settled with the mindset, "this is what I've dealt with for years. I guess I'll always have to deal with this." It is time to pull up a chair to God's dining table. He has prepared a feast for you of His power, His provision, His joy, His peace, His wisdom, His freedom, His healing, and His favor! You have all the power you need!

You have access. You have provision.

Philippians 4:19 (NKJV) says, "God shall supply all your needs according to His riches in Glory by Christ Jesus." You may be going through things in finances, health, business, or marriage. God has given you promises about those things. You have access to all the promises of God.

How do we access these promises? Find the promises in God's Word, pray the promises over your life, and take action towards the promises. Go on a treasure hunt and look for the promises that apply to your need or situation. Begin to pray those promises and then take the steps you know to take. Believe for those promises. Know that you have access to all His promises and provisions!

Lord, I am so thankful that I have access to You through the Holy Spirit. Thank You for supplying all my needs according to your riches in glory (Philippians 4:19). You are my source and I thank You for Your promise of provision in my life. In Jesus name, Amen.

1) Are there some promises that you've forgotten that God has given you? Take time to come boldly to God in prayer for those areas today.

_____

_____

_____

2) Share a time when God provided fully for your situation.

_____

_____

_____

3) Think of the people in your life. Is there an opportunity for you to ask a question, as the other passenger did to the traveler, and help someone discover the provisions they already have access to?

_____

_____

_____

nineteen

Mediocrity →» Authority

Because of Jesus, we have been given authority over the enemy. Jesus said to the disciples in Luke 10:19 (NKJV), "Behold, I give you authority to trample on serpents and scorpions, and over all the power of the enemy, and nothing shall by any means hurt you."

Christ has given you authority as a believer! Authority is delegated power. In this verse when it says, "serpents and scorpions," it's referring to devils and demons—opposition that the enemy would try to bring against you. We don't have to live our lives as a victim to our circumstances or just think, "whatever happens must be the will of God." We can take our God-given authority in prayer.

Matthew 28:18-20 (ESV) shares a moment when Jesus spoke on this saying, "And Jesus came and said to them, 'All authority in heaven and on earth has been given to me. Go therefore and make disciples of all nations, baptizing them in the name of the Father and of the Son and of the Holy Spirit, teaching them to observe all that I have commanded you. And behold, I am with you always, to the end of the age.'" You have authority because Christ is in you, with you, and for you. He has given you a commission, a calling and a purpose to be His representatives in the world!

Recently, I was at home and the doorbell rang. I went to the door and realized I had received a package, so I picked it up and brought it in. I realized it was my favorite coffee and my husband had ordered it as a gift for me. I opened it up and used it. It was delicious! That made me think though. What if I had left the package on the porch? What if I had not opened the box? It might have my name on it, it might be paid for by someone who loves me, but it would have stayed outside the door in the cold and not utilized unless I brought it in, opened it up, used it, and enjoyed the benefits.

The authority God has given us and the promises in His Word work the same way. He has given us an inheritance in His Word of wisdom, revelation, power, provision, grace, but our part is opening up His Word and asking Him to open the eyes of our heart to know Him more and the hope to which He has called us! The package is there. We just have to open the Word, use it, and enjoy the benefits!

The Apostle Paul shared a prayer in Ephesians 1:17-23 (NKJV) that we can pray over our lives, and the lives of others today:

> I pray that the God of our Lord Jesus Christ, the Father of glory, may give to you the spirit of wisdom and revelation in the knowledge of Him [that you would know the person of Jesus], the eyes of your understanding being enlightened [opened]; that you may know what is the hope of His calling [His purpose], what are the riches of the glory of His inheritance in the saints [the provision He has given us], and what is the exceeding greatness of His power toward us who believe [power], according to the working of His mighty power which He worked in Christ when He raised Him from the dead and seated Him at His right hand in the heavenly places, far above all principality and power and might and dominion, and every name that is named, not only in this age but also in that which is to come. And He put all things under His feet and gave Him to be head over all things to the church, which is His body, the fullness of Him who fills all in all (Ephesians 1:17-23 (NKJV)).

There are 4 things that he prayed for believers and they all start with the letter "P," so remember this when you are praying. He prayed that their eyes of their heart would be opened to know the:

1) Person of Christ (personal relationship with Jesus)
2) Purpose of why we were called
3) Provision we have in Christ
4) Power He has given us

I encourage you to pray God's will be done and His kingdom to come in your life, family, and nation wherever you are. Take these scriptures in Ephesians and personalize them.

Lord, I pray that I come to know the person of Christ and the purpose to which I am called. Help me to trust in Your provision for my life and my family's life and help me to be confident knowing that I have power in Christ. In Jesus' name, Amen.

1) Think of a time that you "opened" the gift of authority given to you by Christ. Describe your "aha" moment.

_____

_____

_____

2) What can you do to remember the promises of authority given in Scripture?

_____

_____

_____

3) In what areas of your life do you need to take your God given authority?

_____

_____

_____

twenty

Intimidation →» Boldness

In Acts 3, we read of a time when Peter and John were on their way to the temple to pray. As they went, they met a lame man who had been disabled since birth. When he saw Peter and John, he asked them for money. Peter said, "Silver or gold I do not have, but what I do have I give to you, in the name of Jesus Christ of Nazareth rise up and walk (Acts 3:6 NIV)!"

The man began walking, jumping, and praising God! He was healed. The people were amazed, and then Peter went on to tell the people it was Jesus who healed him. Acts 4:13 points out that when they saw the courage of Peter and John, they realized they had been with Jesus. Boldness comes from being with Jesus.

Several years ago, we took a group of teenagers to Ecuador on a mission trip. In one city, we split up into groups, and when I arrived at the plaza where we were going to set up, there was already another group there. They were all dressed in black, had built altars, and were chanting and calling on evil spirits. Someone in our group suggested that we not disturb them and find another place to minister. I said, "No way, these people need to hear that Jesus is the truth and the only way! They need to hear someone share the life of God—the good news."

We got out and set up our sound system in the plaza, and that other group got upset. They ran over to us yelling and for a brief moment, fear tried to control me, but I knew in my Spirit that we couldn't let fear keep us from the very reason we were there. We began to share the gospel from our corner of the plaza, and a crowd gathered. People were getting saved and healed. Miracles continued to happen, and people shared their healing stories.

After some time, a police officer approached me and asked me to accompany him to the police academy to share this message with the police officers there. We packed up and went with him to an assembly hall with 100 police officers who listened to the good news—and all 100 of them came to the altar to receive Christ. There was, however, one woman in that group who did not, and I approached her with a word from the Lord about her life and she responded that her intentions were to commit suicide that very day. Our message of hope in Christ changed her mind and saved her life.

When I was able to reflect on the events of that day, I was so thankful that I did not let fear and intimidation hold me back. All of those amazing miracles transpired because Jesus gave us the boldness to share His good news with others. As we spend time with Jesus, He gives us boldness to be a witness. Second Timothy 1:7 (NLT) reminds us, "God has not given us a spirit of fear and timidity, but of power, love, and self-discipline."

There are people around us who need Jesus and the hope we have in Christ. This is your time to rise up and be His hands and feet on the earth.

For me, the idea of writing this devotion came as I was walking and praying. I felt the Lord put it on my heart to do, and He's the one who gave me boldness to do it. Remember, "greater is He that is in us than he that is in the world" (1 John 4:4 KJV). Know who is with you—the hope of the world. Spending time with Jesus will produce boldness to tell others about Him. One of the greatest ways we live unstuck is by spending time with Jesus in His word and in prayer. Boldness comes as you are filling yourself up with Him.

When you hang out with Jesus, you become more like him: full of His love and sensitive to His voice when He prompts you to witness or reach out to someone. There are people around us who need Jesus and need the hope we have in Christ. This is your time to rise up and be His hands and feet on the earth. Don't let fear or intimidation hold you back. He tells us plainly, "you will receive power when the Holy Spirit comes on you; and you will be my witnesses in Jerusalem, and in all Judea and Samaria, and to the ends of the earth'" (Acts 1:8 NIV). Spend time with Jesus. Make Him your goal and He will give you boldness which will, in turn, produce results in and through your life.

Lord, help me to be intentional in knowing You so that I can be filled with Your Spirit. Help me to overcome fear and intimidation as I obey you. Give me holy boldness to be a witness wherever I go and carry love, hope, and healing to a broken world. Amen.

1) Think of times when you felt intimidated to share the "good news" of Jesus Christ.

_____

_____

2) What did you learn if you failed to respond to the urge to share?

_____

_____

3) What did you experience when you stepped forward and "did it afraid"?

_____

_____

twenty-one

Complacency →» Action

A s we continue our study, reflect on the ways you have "taken ground" as you have spent time in the Word. I want to encourage you to think of ways you can continue to "take ground" from this point forward in the dreams God has put on your heart. James 2:17 (NIV) says, "Faith by itself, if it is not accompanied by action, is dead."

You may not be able to do the things that were once available to you. However, there might be new things, ideas, or ways of doing things that you can move forward in. In every season, God has direction and guidance for our lives that requires action on our part. It may look different, but there are ways we can take steps of faith.

I remember taking my daughter, Lizzy, to her first swimming lessons when she was little. On the first day of the swimming lesson, the coach walked the kids over to the 10-foot high diving board. He said, "I want you to get a vision of jumping off this high dive and swimming in the deep end by the time you finish these lessons in two weeks." Lizzy turned to me and boldly and confidently said, "I am going to jump off that high dive! You just watch!" She wasn't afraid, (I was the one who was nervous) but she showed me her belief and determination by speaking what she was going to do and then taking steps to get there.

Throughout the week the coach showed them the steps of swimming; how to hold their arms, hold their breath, dive in from the side, and get rings off the bottom of the pool. She got better and better until the final day of the lessons. She left the shallow end, climbed up on that high dive, and jumped off into the deep end!

Many people live in fear of stepping out and doing something because they fear failure, missing it, or worrying about what others will think. Here's the key—start taking steps! Take steps towards your dreams and purpose. The longer you put off responding to what God is leading you to do, the more unsure you will become. Sometimes, we think we are waiting on God, when in reality, God is waiting on us to take steps of faith in what He's already spoken.

This has been true over and over again in my life. God has spoken to us about many things: moving to the mission field, planting a new church, believing God for resources to build our first children's rescue home overseas, and writing a book to name a few. All of these things seemed too big for us to accomplish. Each time it required faith, but as we took steps toward that dream, God began to unfold things, provide resources, and direct us. Not only did God help up move forward, there were people to help on the other side of our obedience.

Start where you are with what you have. You can make a difference!

I encourage you to start taking steps of faith towards the dreams God has given you. They may seem like small steps, but as you step out, you will see how God works. You will see the miraculous way He will provide for your dream. He will connect you to the right people as you are trusting and following His lead. All these things await you after you begin to take steps of faith. You never know the impact of your steps of faith and how they can influence others. With each step of faith, you will gain more and more courage. By the time you take steps to cover the fundamentals, you'll be ready to jump into the deep end from the high dive!

In the military they use the phrase "taking ground" in reference to moving forward and conquering territory; even in sports, the phrase "take ground" is used when they are talking about a team advancing. As I have prayed, I felt the Lord speak this phrase to my heart, for you: this is your year to take ground!

One thing I love about our foundational story of Joshua and Caleb going in to possess the promise land is that in Joshua 13:1, after they had conquered 31 regions and won great victories, the Lord spoke to him and said, "You are now very old and there are still very large areas of land to be taken over." In other words, God was saying, you've taken territory but there is still more I have promised to give you. I love Caleb's response to this. He said, "I am 85 years old, but I am still as strong as the day Moses sent me out; I am just as vigorous to go to battle now as I was then. Now give me this mountain that the Lord has promised me!" (Joshua 14:10b-12). Here's what I want you to get in your spirit: there are still greater things in store for your life and family! God always takes us from faith to faith, glory to glory, and strength to strength!

"God is able to do exceedingly abundantly above all we ask, hope dream or desire according to the power that is at work in us." (Ephesians 3:20 NIV) Think of areas in your life that you are believing to take ground in and write them down:

- In your family

- In your health

- In your finances

- In your marriage

- In your mind

- In the dreams God has put in your heart

- In your community

All throughout the Bible, we see stories of men and women of God who went through different yet difficult seasons. However, as they put their faith in God, He gave them guidance on the steps to take. Whatever that is for you, realize you have what it takes because greater is He that is in you than he that is in the world. Start where you are with what you have. You can make a difference! It's your time to move forward in steps of faith! It's your year to advance!

Lord, I thank You for the dream in my heart. Help me to take the time to take steps of faith, and open my heart to Your direction and the people You will place in my path. I am ready to move forward. Amen.

1) What is the dream God has placed inside your heart? Be specific.

_____

_____

_____

2) What small steps can you take right now towards that dream?

_____

_____

_____

twenty-two

Wandering -» Vision

In Joshua 6, Joshua and the children of Israel were getting ready to enter Jericho. They had just crossed the Jordan River, which was a miracle in itself, and now they were facing the city's great wall. In Joshua 6:2, God told Joshua beforehand, "See! I have given Jericho into your hand" (NKJV).

God began to give Joshua instructions on exactly how to do it. He wanted Joshua to see it on the inside, before he saw it on the outside. Do you see your dreams clearly on the inside? Where is your focus? Are you looking at your problems or how great God is?

We must see our dreams on the inside, before we see them on the outside. We need to keep the vision before us, see with eyes of faith the things God has prepared for us to walk in, and the promises He has given us to possess. God wants to show us things in the spirit that we are called to do and walk in.

**God has given you a divine assignment
to complete for the kingdom.**

So how do we see with eyes of faith? We must fix our eyes on God's Word and meditate on His promises and faithfulness. We must tune out the distractions of the world and focus our heart to hear and see what He is saying. We will always move toward what we focus on.

During the holidays, we planned to take a vacation and told our kids we were going to the beach. We still had a few weeks before leaving, but right away our kids ran, put on their swimsuits, got their towels, and started laying out in the living room. They had already begun to make preparations. They were already imagining themselves at the beach. That's the kind of child-like faith we need—faith that sees what God has in store for us and causes us to prepare ourselves for it. If God has spoken something to you, begin to see yourself walking in that promise by faith and start making preparations for it to come to pass. Ask God to help you see with eyes of faith and let Him show you His strategy for what He wants you to do.

God has unique strategies for you to help fulfill His purpose for your life. He has ways of doing things that haven't been done before. God has a particular way He wants to use you to reach people for His Kingdom.

In Joshua 6:3, God told the children of Israel to march around the wall for seven days, and on the seventh day, to march around seven times, then blow their trumpets and shout. They had never done this before. This might have seemed crazy to some people, but Joshua listened and obeyed what God said. He began to speak to his army and tell them this was how they were going to take over Jericho. He spoke; then they walked it out.

God's Word says if you need wisdom, you can ask Him and He will give it to you (James 1:5). So, if you are wondering what the next step is, just ask God. Seek Him for His divine purpose for your life and how it relates to helping others. Once God gives you that direction or strategy, write it down. Then begin to take the steps necessary to carry it out.

Write down the vision that God put in your heart and release your faith for those things to happen. Remember, you are not being selfish because the dream God has put in you is not just about you. It's about the people you are going to touch and reach. Hang on to it.

Post it on your wall. Declare it. Release your faith for those dreams and visions to come to pass. Habakkuk 2:2 (NKJV) says, "Write the vision and make it plain." After you write it down, start taking steps. Start trusting God. Start doing what He says to do and it will surely come. It won't come in your own might, but, by the grace and power of His Holy Spirit, you can walk out the divine assignment He has called you to walk in.

Another important thing to notice about the battle of Jericho, besides the fact that the Israelites won it, is *how* they won it. They won it through praise. Joshua 6:16 says when they obeyed and shouted to God with the voice of victory, the walls came down.

What walls or obstacles are you up against? Are you believing for healing, direction, or a dream to be fulfilled? Find out what God's Word says about your situation, then speak it and act on what He says to do. When we do what we can do, God can do what only He can do in us and for us, for His glory.

God has given you a divine assignment to complete for the kingdom. But you won't accomplish it if you don't first see it on the inside, begin to call it forth, and then act on what God has said.

Lord, I pray for Your divine direction as I discover the dreams inside of me. I ask for direction as I seek to clarify the vision for my life. Help me to overcome any obstacles that may present themselves. Amen.

1) What is the value of understanding the dreams in your heart and articulating that into a vision?

_____

_____

_____

2) What are some obstacles that you may need to overcome in order to clarify your vision?

_____

_____

_____

3) How does praise release your dream and help expedite vision clarity?

_____

_____

_____

twenty-three

Insecurity →» Knowing Your Value

There is an old story about a man who was visiting a farmer and was surprised to see a beautiful eagle in the farmer's chicken coop. "Why in the world have you got this eagle living in with the chickens?" the man asked.

"Well, I found him when he was little and raised him in there with the chickens. He doesn't know any better. He thinks he is a chicken," the farmer answered.

The man was dumbfounded. The eagle was pecking the grain and drinking from the watering can. The eagle kept his eyes on the ground and strutted around in circles, looking every inch like a big, over-sized chicken.

"Doesn't he ever try to spread his wings and fly out of there?" the man asked.

"No, and I doubt he ever will. He doesn't know what it means to fly," the farmer answered.

"Well, let me take him out and do a few experiments with him," the man said.

The farmer agreed but assured the man that he was wasting his time. The man lifted the bird to the top of the chicken coop fence and said, "Fly!" He pushed the reluctant bird off the fence, and it fell to the ground in a pile of dusty feathers. Next, the man took the ruffled chicken/eagle to the farmer's hayloft and spread its wings before tossing it high in the air again, yelling, "FLY!"

The frightened bird shrieked and fell ungraciously in the barnyard, where it resumed pecking the ground in search of dinner. Again, the man picked up the eagle and decided to give it one more chance, in a more appropriate environment away from the bad example of a chicken's lifestyle. He set the docile bird next to him on the front seat of his pickup truck and headed for the highest cliff in the country.

After a lengthy, sweaty climb to the crest of the cliff with the bird tucked under his arm, he spoke gently to the golden bird. "Friend, you were born to soar. It is better that you die here today on the rocks below than live the rest of your life being a chicken in a pen," he said.

Having said these final words, he lifted the eagle up and once more commanded it to "FLY!" He tossed the bird out into space and this time, much to his relief, it opened its seven-foot wingspan and flew gracefully into the sky. It slowly climbed in spirals into the glare of the morning sun. As crazy as this eagle sounds for not recognizing its true identity, we often do the same thing when we allow others to define our value, simply accepting the label they put on us.

Don't be like the eagle and allow others to define your self-worth or value. You were created by God. You are His masterpiece. You are seated with Christ. You are a child of the King. You have a divine assignment on earth—a holy purpose. Ephesians 2:6-7 (NIV) says, "God raised us up with Christ and seated us with him in heavenly realms in Christ Jesus, in order that in the coming ages he might show the incomparable riches of his grace, expressed in his kindness to us in Christ Jesus." He has called you to rise up and soar above the problems and fears of this world.

If I took a $100 bill and crumpled it up, stomped on it, and threw it in the trash, would it still be worth $100? Yes, of course! If it wasn't completely destroyed, you could still go out and buy something with it. In life, many people have been stepped on, abused, and rejected. Consequently, they assume they have no value. But they are still valuable to God. He paid a great price for all of us—His own Son's life (1 Peter 1:18-19).

Some people judge others by their outward appearance. Others judge them by their education, talent, achievements, or success. But this is the way the world looks at others, not the way God judges a person's value. The Bible says in 2 Corinthians 10:12 that it's not wise to compare yourself with others. God made you for a unique purpose.

I like the way John Mason puts it. He says, "You were born an original. Don't die a copy."[1] The world portrays images of what a man or woman should be. If you look at magazines, TV, or movies, you can see how society tells us how we should look, dress, and talk. Although it is good to try to look our best, the Bible gives us a higher perspective of where our true value lies. God says in Jeremiah 29:11-13 (NIV), "For I know the plans I have for you, declares the Lord, 'plans to prosper you and not to harm you, plans to give you hope and a future. Then you will call upon me … and I will listen to you. You will seek me and find me when you seek me with all your heart.'"

The key to understanding our value and purpose is to seek God first.

For example, if you are a parent and have ever bought a large toy that came with many parts to assemble, you understand the importance of following the instruction manual step-by-step, in order to put it together correctly. I know from experience that when I try to put something together without looking at the manual, I usually mess it up or fail to understand the full function of the item.

---

1 John Mason, "You're Born an Original, Don't Die a Copy!" Insight International, 1993.

Likewise, in our walk with God, in order for us to know our purpose on this earth, we must go back to the instruction manual of our Creator. God is our Creator and His Word is our instruction manual for life. He created us to do great things. Ephesians 2:10 (NIV) says, "For we are God's workmanship, created in Christ Jesus to do good works, which God prepared in advance for us to do."

Joyce Meyer shares about how her father sexually abused her 200 times, from when she was a young girl, until she was 18 years old. She grew up in fear and shame, not knowing her true value. But as she got into God's Word, she began to understand God's love for her and received healing and restoration in her heart. She began to understand that God had a purpose for her life. She renewed her mind with the Word of God. Now she is on television every day, preaching the Gospel all over the world and sharing the life changing power of God's Word.

Psalm 139 says that God knew you in your mother's womb. He made you, and His thoughts of you are more than the grains of sand. He knows every hair on your head. So, don't compare yourself with others. God made you unique for a purpose. He put specific gifts and talents on the inside of you.

You are not a mistake. You are not an accident. The circumstances surrounding your birth may not have been ideal, but God meant for you to be here. God knows you by name. He knows how many hairs are on your head. He cares about you and has a great purpose for your life. In fact, 1 Corinthians 2:9-10 in the Message Bible says that what God has arranged for you is beyond your imagination, but He promises to reveal that purpose to you by His Spirit.

Another man, James Robinson, has a worldwide TV ministry that also touches millions of people. He was born, as what some would consider a "mistake," because his mother was raped. But God still had a plan for his life. Today, his ministry feeds millions of hungry children in Africa because he chose to believe God had a purpose for his life.

First Peter 2:9 (NIV) says, "You are a chosen people, a royal priest-hood, a holy nation, a people belonging to God, that you may declare the praises of him who called you out of darkness into his wonderful light." You are a royal child of the King. You are called to declare His praises. And you can make a difference in the lives of others.

So why did God make you the way you are? Why are you here at this time in history? You are here now, just the way you are, because God knew the world would need you. You have talents and abilities the world needs. When you realize God loves you and has a purpose for you, your life will take on a whole new meaning. You are called to make a difference in the lives of others, no matter where you live or work.

Lord, thank You that I am here on purpose because I have a purpose. I am fearfully and wonderfully made. I am Your workmanship created for good works that You prepared in advance for me to walk in. Thank You for opening my eyes to my part in the body of Christ. In Jesus' name, Amen.

1) What are some circumstances from your history that may have caused you to question your value?

_____

_____

_____

2) How did you overcome those thoughts? If you haven't yet, take the time to re-read this entry and accompanying Scripture so that you can begin to fully grasp the importance of who You are to God.

_____

_____

_____

3) How can you use your circumstances to help others?

_____

_____

_____

twenty-four

Shame → Freedom

Galatians 5:1 (NIV) says, "It is for freedom that Christ has set us free. Stand firm then and do not let yourselves be burdened again by a yoke of slavery."

After we get saved, we are forgiven, cleansed, and free, but can still deal with thoughts and feelings of shame. The enemy loves to heap shame on you and try to get you to identify with who you were in the past. You may still be dealing with negative labels people have put on you or lies of the enemy in your mind saying things like you are:

- Unworthy

- Worthless

- A Liar

- Rejected

- Depressed

- Impure

- Fearful

- Stupid

- Not good enough

Think about what labels you have accepted about yourself that are contrary to the Word. Here's how I want to encourage you today: you don't have to let those labels stick!

When you receive Christ, He cleanses you from your past sins and gives you His righteousness. Imagine an old, dirty, torn coat being taken off of you, and someone giving you a new, clean one in its place. That is what Christ has done for us on the cross. Second Corinthians 5:21 tells us that in Christ we are made righteous. *Righteous* means right standing with God.

The Bible continues to say that the old things (sin and shame) are passed away and all things have become new. We must wake up and realize that we are no longer a slave to sin, guilt, and shame. We can live alive to righteousness and God's purpose for our lives. Ephesians 4:22-24 (NIV) says, "Put off concerning your former conduct, the old man which grows corrupt according to the deceitful lusts, and be renewed in the spirit of your mind, and that you put on the new man which was created according to God, in true righteousness and holiness." I like the way Romans 13:14 in the Message translation puts it, it says, "Dress yourselves in Christ." How do we dress ourselves in Christ? By renewing our mind with what His Word says about us.

One of the ladies who is now in our home church had been through a lot of hurt in her past from her father, and chose to look to drugs to numb the pain she was feeling as a result. She went from using drugs to selling drugs, and subsequently ended up being caught and thrown in jail. She shares that while she was in jail, the Lord appeared to her in her jail cell and told her how much He loved her, and that He had a better plan for her life. She fell to her knees and gave her heart to Jesus. She told the Lord she would never go back to the old ways again and committed to living her life for Christ. Miraculously, she was released early, and began coming to church and enrolled in Bible school. As she renewed her mind with the Word, she began to realize who God said she was. She chose to receive the love of God, forgive her father, and throw off the lies of shame. She became so on fire for God that she would witness to everyone she came in contact with. It has now been over 15 years since she was saved. Today, she is one of the leaders in our church and coordinates the evangelism teams in sharing the truth of God's Word with others of how they can be free. Her life is making an impact because she chose to move forward from shame into Christ's freedom!

Here is what I want you to realize: You are not defined by your past or by what others say. You are defined by your Creator.

You are defined by who you are in Christ.

You can replace the negative labels by meditating on who God says about you. The way to go to the next level in what He is asking you to do is to meditate on the Word of God and gain a greater revelation of who you are in Christ. His Word will empower you to walk out His perfect will for your life.

You can meditate on Scriptural truths like these for encouragement:

- I am the righteousness of God in Christ Jesus. (2 Corinthians 5:21)

- I am no longer a slave to sin. (Galatians 2:4)

- I am forgiven, accepted, and chosen because of Jesus. (Ephesians 1-2)

- I have the mind of Christ. (1 Corinthians 2:16)

- I can do all things through Christ who strengthens me. (Philippians 4:13)

- I am loved. (1 John 4:10)

- I am complete in Christ. (Colossians 2:10)

- I am anointed. (1 John 2:20)

- I am wonderfully made. (Psalm 139:14)

- I am created for good works. (Ephesians 2:10)

- I have the mind of Christ. (1 Corinthians 2:16)

- I am peaceful. (Philippians 4:7)

- I am chosen. (1 Peter 2:9)

- I am free (Galatians 5:1)

- I am healed. (1 Peter 2:24)

- I am empowered. (Acts 1:8)

- I am blessed. (Philippians 4:19)

As you meditate on these promises, you will receive a revelation of God's love for you, along with the freedom you have in Him. Today, renew your mind to who you are in Christ and speak what He says about yourself, your life, your family, your children! God's word is powerful and gives us the power to walk in victory!

> *Lord, Your Word contains the truth of who I am in You. Help me to focus on who You say that I am. Help me to break free from shame and lose this heavy burden that keeps me from advancing. Thank You that I am the righteousness of God in Christ Jesus. Amen.*

1) How is it possible for shame to hold you down with its heavy reminders?

_____

_____

_____

2) Write out three of the Scriptures that spoke to your thoughts and heart.

   1. _____

   2. _____

   3. _____

3) What are some practical ways that you can daily renew your mind?

_____

_____

_____

twenty-five

Anxiety → Trust

Many of us deal with feeling stuck, restarting in different areas of life, or experiencing events beyond our control that impact us. Moving forward in faith in your journey will require a break from anxiety and putting your trust in God. Proverbs 12:25 (NASB) says, "anxiety in a man's heart weighs it down, but a good word makes it glad." Anxiety weighs our hearts down and can even cause depression. It keeps us from moving forward.

Anxiety is a toxic cycle of thoughts becoming worries and worries becoming thoughts.

One of the biggest areas I had to learn to trust God in was believing for the right husband. When I went to college, I was so excited to meet new people. I was at a Christian university and thought, for sure, I would meet my husband there. During the first few weeks, the Lord spoke to my heart not to date during my first year. I thought, *"What?! God, I've been waiting so long already. I thought I was going to find my man of God at college."* I was worried that I would miss the right guy for me, or he would miss me if I wasn't available.

During my first semester, I was asked to be a chaplain in my dorm, and my dad also asked me to be one of the children's pastors in a new service they were starting at our church. In addition to that, I had a part-time job in the Alumni Office on campus, and worked part-time at a local store. I knew the Lord wanted me to focus on what He had put in my hands, instead of looking for a guy.

It wasn't easy though, because a guy at my school started pursuing me. I began to think, *"He is popular. He is such a great guy. Everyone says I should date him."* I was flattered and thought that if I didn't date him, I would lose him to some other girl. I became impatient and started dating him anyway.

I dated him for two years, and we even started serving at the church together. When he asked me to marry him, I didn't have complete peace but thought it was just pre-wedding jitters, so I said, "yes."

Ten days before the wedding, things really came to a head, and both of us realized we did not have peace about getting married at that time. It was a hard decision to make, but I decided to call it off completely. Afterwards, I asked God what I did wrong in the process and He brought me back to the beginning—I didn't obey His voice when he said wait. The Lord began to deal with me about not trusting Him with that area of my heart. I was impatient and rushing ahead because I was afraid I would miss out.

So, I am speaking from experience when I encourage you to trust God with your relationships. Don't rush or compromise. One of the verses I have clung to is in Matthew 6:33 in the Message Bible. It says, "Don't worry about missing out. You will find your everyday human concerns will be met. Give your entire attention to what God is doing right now, and don't get worked up about what may or may not happen tomorrow. God will help you deal with whatever hard things come up when the time comes." Keep God's Word first in your life. It is your compass.

After waiting a year and a half after that breakup, my future husband, Caleb, began to pursue me. We had been friends since high school and during that time we had gone on a mission trip to Africa. On that trip, Caleb surrendered his life to Jesus and to the call of God to work in the ministry. He told me that during that trip he knew he wanted to marry me, but he didn't say anything because he realized he wasn't ready. He made a decision to prepare himself and seek God's purpose for His life.

Six years after that trip, when we went on our first date, he shared his heart and the vision he had for his life with me. It was like I met him for the first time. It was as if he was reading my heart to me. He had been volunteering at church all those years, getting trained and focusing on God. He became a new man.

Our heart and passion for the Lord were in sync. Our focus on the call God had for us to the nations matched. I realized he was everything I had prayed for, and there was an overwhelming peace that we were both at a place in which we were ready for marriage. I discovered firsthand the truth in Ecclesiastes 3:11, "God makes all things beautiful in His time."

Anxiety is a toxic cycle of thoughts becoming worries and worries becoming thoughts. Focusing on the negatives of life can open the door to this cycle of anxiety, and it can be very burdensome and heavy. You may feel burdened with all the cares of life, wondering about the future, about your family, about your health, or about your finances. But I want to encourage you to trust God completely because He is the Creator of the Universe. He's the Creator of your life. He has good plans for you. You can trust Him with your life. You don't have to be in constant fear about where you are headed.

Proverbs 3:5-6 (NKJV) says, "Trust in the Lord with all your heart, lean not on your own understanding, in all your ways acknowledge Him and He will direct your path." The word, "ways", in that verse, is also translated in all your "days" acknowledge Him. As we daily come to the Lord, and put our trust in Him, He will direct us.

Let this be an encouragement to you that you can break free from anxiety and move forward in trust as you bring your concerns to God daily. Let His peace guard your heart and mind in Christ Jesus. He is our source and He is able to direct our steps.

> *Lord, help me to cast my cares on You. Help me to trust that You will take care of me and that Your Word will not return void. Give me the strength to release negative thoughts and burdens to You so that I can be full of peace as I move forward for all You have for me. Amen.*

1) Identify the cares that have been weighing you down.

_____

_____

_____

2) Pray over each of them, making sure to leave that concern with God for the answer.

3) Which of the Scripture(s) above spoke to you? Write it down and place it somewhere that you can be reminded of that truth often.

_____

_____

_____

twenty-six

Struggle → Surrender

When I was in the sixth grade, I joined the girls' basketball team—not because I liked playing basketball, but because my dad liked it and I wanted to please him. I didn't know much about the game or the rules, but I showed up at the first game with my jersey on, thinking I could just "wing it." The sixth-grade boys had played right before us and Caleb, who is now my husband, was their star basketball player. When it was the girls turn to play, hundreds of fans were gathered on the bleachers in expectation of a great game. I remember sitting on the bench, and halfway through the game the coach called my name to go in the game. My heart was beating so fast; I quickly ran onto the court. I thought, "*If I just run back and forth, it will look like I know what is going on.*"

Suddenly, the ball was thrown to me. The only thing I knew to do was run as fast as I could to the goal and try to score a point. I was surprised, as I was running that I had such a clear path to the basket, and then "swoosh"—I made a basket! I was so happy! I jumped up and down, screaming. Even I was surprised that I had made the basket! But as I looked at my teammates, I realized I had made a big mistake. No one else was clapping except for the fans of our opposing team. I had made a basket for the other team! I did not have a clue which goal I needed to be aiming for. I was devastated as a sixth grader seeing all of my classmates laughing at me. Middle school is hard enough, right?!

Thankfully, Caleb didn't hold it against me, and he sure didn't marry me for my basketball skills.

Sometimes we can be aiming at the wrong goal in life. There are times that God reminds me of that embarrassing moment and says, "Sarah, what is your goal? Who are you seeking to please?" He lovingly reassures me, "If you will seek to please Me and obey Me, then I will lead you into My best."

He is the goal. Knowing Him, pleasing Him, and following His plan is the goal. The most important thing is keeping a living connection with Jesus on a daily basis. The Apostle Paul brings us into focus on what is important in Philippians 3. He was a man who had all kinds of worldly accomplishments, accolades, degrees, and titles, but he came to a place where he said, "All the things that I once thought were so important are gone from my life [the accomplishments, position, status]. Compared to the high privilege of knowing Christ Jesus as my Master, firsthand everything I once thought I had going for me is insignificant—dog dung. I've dumped it all in the trash so that I could embrace Christ" Philippians 3:7 (MSG).

He is the goal. The most important thing is keeping a living connection with Jesus on a daily basis.

He goes on to say in Philippians 3:10-14 (NIV):

> *I want to know Christ—yes, to know the power of His resurrection and participation in His sufferings, becoming like Him in His death, and so, somehow, attaining to the resurrection from the dead. Not that I have already obtained all this, or have already arrived at my goal, but I press on to take hold of that for which Christ Jesus took hold of me. Brothers and sisters, I do not consider myself yet to have taken hold of it. But one thing I do: Forgetting what is behind and straining toward what is ahead, I press*

on toward the goal to win the prize for which God has called me heaven-
ward in Christ Jesus.

Above everything else, status, fame, accomplishments, and ministry, Paul said his number one goal was to know Jesus, to love Him, and to reach after His high calling for his life. I think it's important to evaluate our lives and focus on a regular basis. It's easy for our priorities to get out of order because of the demands of life, and challenges that we all face. Right now, during this season, we can shift our focus, taking time to evaluate and prioritize what matters most.

A.W. Tozer said it best when he said, "When God is at the center, a thousand problems are solved at once."[2] One of the greatest ways we break free from struggling or striving in our flesh is to surrender to God and seek Him first. Matthew 6:33 (NKJV) says, "Seek first the kingdom of God and His righteousness and all these things shall be added to you." According to Scripture, if we seek Him first, He will add the things we need.

I want to encourage you to surrender your life to Him. Make Him your goal. Surrender your expectations and your plans to God in prayer and ask for His will to be done. Trust that He is working in your life for good. As you seek Him first, He'll add the things that you need, you'll experience supernatural peace, and receive clarity on your next step.

> *Lord, as I meditate on Your Word, thank you for strengthening*
> *me. I choose to seek you first above all else. Remind me of the*
> *goals that are worth focusing on and achieving. Amen.*

1) Why is it so important to aim at a God-given goal?

_____

_____

_____

2 A.W. Tozer, "The Pursuit of God," 1957

2) Have you ever aimed at the wrong goal, hit your target, then realized it was all wrong? Share that experience here.

_____

_____

_____

3) How can you evaluate your priorities regularly to ensure that you are being fully obedient and surrendered to God's will?

_____

_____

_____

twenty-seven

Old Habits →» Renewal

There is a story of an old man who lived high above an Austrian village along the slopes of the Alps. The town council hired this old man as "the keeper of the spring," to maintain the purity of the pools of water in the mountain crevices. The overflow from these pools of water ran down the mountainside and fed the lovely spring that flowed through the town.

Faithfully and quietly, the keeper of the spring patrolled the hills, removing the leaves and branches and wiping away the silt that would contaminate the fresh flow of water. As time went on, the village became a popular attraction for vacationers, the water was beautiful, and the farmlands were naturally irrigated.

Years passed. One evening, the town council met for its semi-annual meeting. As the council members reviewed the budget, one man's eye caught the salary paid to the keeper of the spring. He asked, "Who is this old man? Why do we keep paying him year after year? No one ever sees him. For all we know, this man does us no good. He isn't necessary any longer."

By a unanimous vote, the council fired the man. For several weeks nothing changed. But by early autumn, the trees began to shed their leaves and small branches began to fall into the pools, hindering the flow of water. One afternoon, someone noticed a yellowish-brown tint in the water. A few days later, it had darkened even more. The mill wheels eventually stopped moving. Businesses near the water closed. Tourists no longer wanted to visit the town. Eventually, disease spread within the village.

The town council realized the importance of guarding the water source, so they hired the man back, and over a few weeks, the water was restored to its purity. Like the keeper of the spring, we are the keeper of our heart. Proverbs 4:23 (KJV) says, "Above all else guard your heart, for out of it flows the issues of life." What will help us stay fresh and flourishing every day? Continually renewing our minds with His Word. Romans 12:1-2 (MSG) makes it clear:

> So, here's what I want you to do, God helping you: Take your everyday, ordinary life—your sleeping, eating, going-to-work, and walking-around life—and place it before God as an offering. Embracing what God does for you is the best thing you can do for him. Don't become so well-adjusted to your culture that you fit into it without even thinking. Instead, fix your attention on God. You'll be changed from the inside out. Readily recognize what he wants from you, and quickly respond to it. Unlike the culture around you, always dragging you down to its level of immaturity, God brings the best out of you, develops well-formed maturity in you.

The New King James Translation of this passage reads this way: "Do not be conformed to this world, but be transformed by renewing your mind" (Romans 12:2 KJV). Daily, there is so much "junk" that tries to pollute our hearts, such as bitterness, envy, jealousy, fear, lust, and self-pity. That's why we need to continually be transformed by renewing our mind with God's Word. Then we will know the perfect will of God.

The word renew means to make new again, to bring back into good condition, to give new spiritual strength, to restore, refresh, revive, rebuild and rejuvenate.

Vines Dictionary defines renewing your mind as, "the adjustment of the moral and spiritual vision and thinking to the mind of God."

Have you ever used the Internet, walked away, and then when you came back to the computer, you realized you needed to hit the refresh button to update the web page you were on? Why? Because what you saw on your screen may actually have been an outdated page. Since the Internet is constantly reloading, you want to be sure you are viewing up-to-date information. Every day, God wants to refresh and renew our spirits. To refresh means to make clean, revive, give new vigor or spirit to. The word refresh implies the supplying of something necessary to restore lost strength, animation, or power. There is a refueling that takes place in the presence of God. Your natural ability can only take you so far, but as you wait on God and spend time in His presence, He will renew your strength and give you fresh insight in the areas that you need it.

Have you ever been in a battle where your spirit wants to follow after God, but your flesh wants to go in another direction? Your spirit wants to do things for Him and wants to be obedient to whatever He says, but if your flesh has been fed a little bit more than your spirit, the flesh will dominate every time. The flesh will win out because it's a lot stronger.

Every day, God wants to refresh and renew our spirits.

So many Christians battle with this tug-of-war between the flesh and spirit on the inside. Some have struggled with thoughts of fear, lust, perversion, or addiction. Others have struggled with hatred toward someone, and the battle inside them has caused them to hold onto resentment. But if we seek the secret place with God, we will find His strength and power to win that battle.

How do you overcome temptations or things that have you bound? First of all, you can repent and remove wrong influences and mindsets. Then you must replace those wrong thoughts with what God's Word says about your life. It takes discipline to renew your mind, but it is worth it to experience the freedom that Christ has already paid for. As you feed your spirit with the Word of God, it will get stronger and will be able to overcome the temptations of the flesh.

"Out of your heart flows the issues of life" (Proverbs 4:23 KJV). Out of your heart, flows your thoughts, your words, and your actions. When the tug-of-war comes into your mind and tries to allow negativity into your heart, begin to speak and mediate on the Word. It will strengthen you so that you can say no to those temptations. Like physical strengthening, this strengthening is a continual process, but you will see the reward of your decisions.

Right before Joshua took the Israelites into the promised land, the area that they had been striving to get to for 40 long years, the Lord stopped him and gave him the secret to having a successful life. In Joshua 1:8, He says, "This Book of the Law shall not depart from your mouth, but you shall meditate in it day and night, that you may observe to do according to all that is written in it. For then you will make your way prosperous, and then you will have good success. Have I not commanded you? Be strong and of good courage; do not be afraid, nor be dismayed, for the Lord your God is with you wherever you go."

Joshua was an incredible man of faith. I admire him because against all odds, he stayed in a spirit of faith. He led the children of Israel into the promised land because he chose to meditate on the Word day and night. He chose to renew his mind with God's word and make it a priority in his life.

As you meditate on the Word, you will have fresh strength for every single day. You will have the grace to overcome the temptations and battles that come into your mind, and you will walk in the new things that God has called you to do. In addition, God's Word will cause you to flourish. The word flourish means to grow well, to thrive, to be in a place of influence, to be successful, prosperous, generous, and producing good fruit. God has not just called you to survive but to thrive!

Lord, thank You as I renew my mind with Your Word, You are transforming me into Your image. Thank You, Lord, for Your grace that is enough to help me overcome any temptations or challenges that I might face. Amen.

1) Can you identify a few pieces of "junk" in your heart that may be blocking the flow of God's presence? Write those here and some Scriptures that apply that can help you in the process of renewal.

_____

_____

_____

2) What are some tangible and intangible benefits to releasing negativity from your mind as you renew and refresh?

_____

_____

_____

twenty-eight

Temporal → Eternal

James 4:14 describes our life on earth as being like a vapor or mist that is visible for a little while, but then disappears. When we live with eternity in mind, we will more readily reach out with the love of God to those who have not heard the Gospel.

When I was 13 years old, our house caught on fire in the middle of the night. My dad's back had been hurting at night, so he slept in the guest room where there was a firm mattress. Also, that night I decided to sleep in my mom's room with her, which was rare for me.

At 2:00 a.m., my dad began to hear beeping sounds. He woke up and discovered the house was filled with smoke. He began to yell and scream, "Wake up! Wake up! Get out of the house! The house is on fire!" As we woke up, we couldn't see well because of all the smoke. Still, my dad, mom, my brother John, and I managed to get out of the house.

After we got out and turned around, we realized that my sister, Ruthie, and my youngest brother, Paul, were still in the house. My dad's eyes had already been burned from the fire, but he bravely went back in and found Ruthie and pulled her out. Then, he went back in for the second time to find my brother Paul, who was only six years old at the time. He was on his hands and knees on the door in the hallway waiting for someone to come and get him. My dad felt his head, grabbed him by the shirt collar, and pulled him out.

When we all got out and began to run across the street, the front of the house where we had been standing burst into flames. The entire house was consumed, and when the firemen came, they were expecting to pull dead bodies out of the house. They asked whose room was closest to where the fire originated, and I realized it was my room. The firemen proceeded to inform us that due to the location of my room, if I had been in there, I would have been trapped and probably would not have made it out. It was definitely a miracle that we all got out safely.

None of us ever forgot my dad's bravery and love he displayed to us that night. He ended up being hospitalized for a couple weeks after the incident due to damaged eyesight, but he didn't care. He didn't care about his eyes being burned nearly as much as he did about getting all of us out of that burning house. In the hospital he just kept saying, "I got everyone out! I got everyone out! They are all saved!"

We must wake up to the urgency of the hour we are living in today.

This story always reminds me of our responsibility as believers. It's easy to get so concerned with what others think about us or how we appear that we don't take the time to tell them that they are asleep in a "burning house," so to speak. There are people who are lost and going to hell without the knowledge of Jesus, and we have the opportunity to bring them the truth. I don't say this to bring heaviness to you, but rather an awareness of their eternal destination without Christ.

We must wake up to the urgency of the hour we are living in today. Jude 1:21-23 (NIV) says, "Keep yourselves in God's love as you wait for the mercy of our Lord Jesus Christ to bring you to eternal life. Be merciful to those who doubt; snatch others from the fire and save them."

We are called as Christ's ambassadors to fulfill a divine assignment: to share God's message of hope, healing, and love with the world in whatever field of work we are in. Hebrews 10:24 tells us that as we see the day of the Lord approaching, we should see how inventive we can be in encouraging love and good works (MSG).

There are opportunities we pass every day to share the love of Jesus. We must listen to His still, small voice and be obedient to the promptings He gives us to reach out to those in need. There have been times that I have missed opportunities and have had to repent for being too busy or selfish to stop. On the other hand, I have also experienced the most amazing times in the presence of God after a moment of stopping to share the love of Jesus with someone in need. When we reach out to those in need, we are actually spending time with Jesus. In these moments, we begin to hear His heartbeat—people.

Several times, I have heard the story of a young boy who was walking along the beach and noticed thousands of starfish washed up on the shore. He knew they would die if they were left out of the water, so he began to pick them up, one by one, and throw them back in the ocean. An older man came by and asked him, "What are you doing?" He replied, "I'm saving the starfish! If I don't throw them in, they will die!"

The old man said, "Son, there are miles of beach and thousands of star fish. What makes you think it really makes a difference?" The boy listened for a moment, and then picked one up and said, "It makes a difference to this one." After that, the old man joined the young boy to help save the starfish.

Sometimes we think that our little part doesn't make a difference, but it does. We can make a difference one person at a time. There are opportunities in our church, community, and world to get involved and be a light.

God is calling us to wake up out of depression, fear, and hurt. He's calling us to rise up to the divine assignment He has for us and to walk in His love toward others. There are people all around us who need this, so let's use the freedom Christ has given us to live a life of love.

Think about the people that are in your sphere of influence that you can reach out to. Make a list of those that God puts on your heart to pray for and then take a step of faith to share the love of Jesus with them. You never know how one moment of your time could mean eternity to someone else!

Lord, ignite a sense of urgency in my heart so that I may share Your love with those around me in order to help others come to know You. Give me boldness to follow Your direction. Amen.

1) Share your experience of coming to know Jesus. How did you realize how temporary this life is?

_____

_____

_____

2) How can you help others feel "seen" like the miles of starfish? How can you reach out to one?

_____

_____

_____

3) As you read this entry, who came to your mind? Write a plan to reach out to those individuals today.

_____

_____

_____

twenty-nine

Former Things →» New Things

When I became pregnant with my first child, my stomach started to stretch in order to accommodate the growing baby inside. I felt like I expanded more than I wanted to! Those of you that have had babies know that when you conceive and carry a baby, it's not comfortable, but you know it's worth it because you are bringing forth NEW LIFE. In the same way, any time you want to grow in an area of your life, you will be stretched. Whenever God gives new vision, it will cause us to be stretched in our faith. It's like having a baby.

God wants to birth new things in you and in His church, but it will require you to be stretched in your faith. It will cause you to depend on God more than ever because, apart from Him, we can do nothing that will produce fruit.

Consider the imagery of a bow and arrow. An archer or hunter will take an arrow, place it methodically into the string of a bow, pull back with great strength, aim precisely at their target, then carefully release the arrow, and it launches forward. When it's stretched back, there is tension, but that tension helps it to be propelled! Maybe you've felt like you've been in hiding or pulled back. You may feel tense, stretched, and tired. Maybe the enemy has tried to bring attacks against your life—but God can turn those things around for your good. Sometimes when we are stretched, it's the only way we grow. Embrace the stretch of faith and realize God is about ready to propel you into something greater!

Isaiah 43:18-19 (NKJV) says, "Do not remember the former things, nor consider the things of old. Behold, I will do a new thing, now it shall spring forth… I will even make a road in the wilderness and rivers in the desert." God wants to do a new thing in your life, but you must make room for Him to move. Life can get so full of distractions and sin that it weighs you down and stops you from receiving the new things He is trying to give you.

When we were in the process of selling our home and packing up to move to the mission field, I realized we had accumulated a lot of unnecessary stuff (junk). Our garage was full of stuff we had to sort through and get rid of. In fact, when we finally left to go on the mission field, we only brought eight suitcases for all four of us (not including two car seats). I realized there were a lot of things that were unnecessary for us to take to our new place. It was more expensive and more trouble for us to take most of the old things we had, than to just get new things when we got there.

Spiritually speaking, it's the same way. Many times, we try to hang on to the old things—old habits and old mindsets—but those things will only slow us down when we go where God wants to take us. He wants us to lay those things down so there will be room for Him to do a *new thing* in our lives and use us to help others.

Paul said in Philippians 3:13 (NIV), "One thing I do: Forgetting what is behind and straining toward what is ahead, I press on toward the goal to win the prize for which God has called me heavenward in Christ Jesus." The Message translations says, "Friends, don't get me wrong: By no means do I count myself an expert in all of this, but I've got my eye on the goal, where God is beckoning us onward—to Jesus. I'm off and running, and I'm not turning back."

None of us have arrived. None of us are perfect. But we can still follow Paul's example and forget the things that are behind: our past failures, offenses, and other things that have held us back. We can reach forward to the new things that God has for us and to the call He has on our lives.

The key is to start taking steps! God does not need us to *feel* ready to do what He has called us to do. He wants us to trust Him and step out in faith!

I believe today, as you begin taking steps of faith, you will see doors begin to open. It will be like the automatic doors they have in many buildings now. As you take a step the sensor sees it and the doors open! I've found that many times, you won't see the favor, provision, or open doors until you start taking steps, so today, step out, and find out the new things God has in store for you!

Lord, I eagerly look forward to what is ahead! Help me let go of the things that are holding me back and seek out the steps I need to take in order to fulfill Your purpose in my life. Amen.

1) What are some "former things" or mindsets that may be holding you back that you need to let go of?

_____

_____

_____

2) What are some areas where God is currently stretching you to step out in new things?

_____

_____

_____

3) Write down three areas of your life where you are believing God to propel you into something greater:

1. _____

_____

2. _____

_____

3. _____

_____

thirty

Limitation –» Wide Open Spaces

A s we are concluding our journey of advancement, I want to encourage
you to take the limits off your faith and believe God for greater things!
Through this process, you have spent time seeking after God by allowing
this message to direct you to His Word and to pray earnestly. You have been
stretched, and I pray that you are poised to propel forward in advancement
into wide open spaces.

In 2 Corinthians 6:11-13 (MSG) God reveals a hope that He has for us when
He says, "… I long for you to enter the wide-open spacious life… we didn't
fence you in… live openly and expansively." God wants you to break free from
any self-imposed limitations.

When I went to Thailand to speak at a women's conference, I stayed at the
mission base of a fellow missionary and friend. Since I enjoy running in the
mornings, they told me that I could go outside the compound in the morning
to run around the block. I was excited because Thailand is a beautiful country
with mountains all around and many sites to explore.

The next morning, I woke up and got ready to take a jog. But when I went to the gate, it was locked. I went to the other side, but it was also locked. I was fenced in, but I was ready to run. It was early and I didn't want to wake anyone up, so I just sat there at the gate. The Lord began to speak to me, and He showed me that there are many times that there are things He has called us to do, but we have "self-imposed" gates that are locked.

The Bible says we were created for good works that we should walk in, but sometimes we are "fenced in" or held back because of fear, discouragement, apathy, or selfishness. The Lord began to speak to me about the importance of taking the "limits off" of my faith and believing He can do greater things through believers to reach more people with His love and bring Him glory in the earth. I encourage you to do the same. He is able to do above and beyond what we could imagine. Nothing is impossible with Him.

Another thing happened while I was on that specific trip to Thailand. We had finished our ministry time and took the team we brought to ride elephants. It was so much fun, but something I noticed afterwards was that these huge creatures were being held by only a small rope tied to their front leg. No chains, no cages. It was obvious that the elephants could, at any time, break away from their bonds but for some reason, they did not. We found out that if they are caught when they are very young, these elephants will have that small sized rope tied on them and, at that age, it's enough to hold them. As they grow up, they are conditioned to believe they cannot break away. They believe the rope can still hold them, so they never try to break free.

These animals could, at any time, break free from their ropes, but because they believed they couldn't, they were stuck right where they were. Like the elephants, many times people have been set free, but are living in fear and won't step out into the wide-open spaces of grace and possibilities because of the lies of the enemy.

Don't let the enemy get you into a limited mindset or a stagnant mindset. It's easy to get comfortable in things God has already done, feeling like we have enough, "for us four and no more." But we must continue to believe for more.

Our faith is not just for ourselves; it's for the people we are called to reach. When God moves in our lives, people are influenced, and God is glorified.

Even when our world faced a major pandemic that brought life as we knew it to a halt, the Lord continued to speak these words to my heart: "You are entering wide open spaces of My grace." This passage in Romans 5:1-2 (MSG) came to my mind: "We throw open our doors to God and discover at the same moment that he has already thrown open his door to us. We find ourselves standing where we always hoped we might stand—out in the wide-open spaces of God's grace and glory, standing tall and shouting our praise."

Our faith is not just for ourselves; it's for the people we are called to reach.

Sometimes we think God can only use those who are called into full time ministry, but that is not what the word of God says. God has called His people to be a light in every sector of society—in business, government, media, arts, communication, family and education. He has called you to lift Him up with the gifts, talents, and opportunities you have.

For the sake of the people on the other side, you must live a life of faith and love. There are people who need what you have. Don't hold back. When we are motivated by love and operate in faith, miracles happen. You may be called to step out in new things, but it might be uncomfortable. You may feel like you don't know how to do it, but as you take one step at a time, God will give you the next step to take. I believe today you are breaking free from limitations and moving forward into the wide open spaces of God's favor! This is your time to advance!

Lord, help me recognize my self-imposed barriers that prevent me from moving into Your wide-open spaces. I want to reach forward to impact those around me. Give me the next steps. Amen.

1) Think about the "limitations" in the natural or in your mind or heart that might be holding you back. What are the "limits" that have tried to hold you back, and how can you move forward in the wide-open spaces of God's grace?

_____

_____

_____

2) Take some time to meditate on these passages:
   - Psalm 119:45-46 says "I'll stride freely through wide open spaces as I look for your truth and your wisdom; Then I'll tell the world what I find, speak out boldly in public, unembarrassed."
   - 2 Samuel 22:20 says, "He also brought me forth into a broad place; He rescued me, because He delighted in me."
   - Psalm 31:8 says, "You have not given me over into the hand of the enemy; You have set my feet in a large place."

3) In Prayer today, ask God to show you the wide-open spaces he has opened for you and believe that He is making a way where there seems to be no way!

Salvation Prayer

As you have read this book, my prayer is that you have gained a greater revelation of God's love for you. No matter who you are, no matter what your past, God loves you so much that He gave His one and only begotten Son for you. The Bible tells us that "… everyone who believes in him will not perish but have eternal life" (John 3:16 NLT). Jesus laid down His life and rose again so that we could spend eternity with Him in heaven and experience His absolute best on earth. If you would like to receive Jesus into your life, pray this prayer out loud and mean it from your heart.

Heavenly Father, I come to You admitting that I am a sinner. Right now, I choose to turn away from sin, and I ask You to cleanse me of all unrighteousness. I believe that Your Son, Jesus, died on the cross to take away my sins. I also believe that He rose again from the dead so that I might be forgiven of my sins and be made righteous through faith in Him. I call upon the name of Jesus Christ to be the Savior and Lord of my life. Jesus, I choose to follow You and ask that You fill me with the power of the Holy Spirit. I declare that right now I am a child of God. I am free from sin and full of the righteousness of God. I am saved in Jesus' name. Amen.

About the Author

Sarah Wehrli is a passionate speaker and author currently serving as the Executive Director of Inspire International, a mission organization with a focus on evangelizing the lost, equipping leaders, and bringing practical relief to orphans and children at risk globally. Sarah has ministered in 40 different countries over the past 20 years. She previously spent time with her family as a missionary in Hong Kong. She has served in multiple areas of church leadership at Victory Church in Tulsa, Oklahoma, USA, and she has helped pioneer church planting and missions initiatives around the globe. Sarah is passionate about connecting people to their unique purpose in life and helping them experience God in a real way. Sarah has a theology degree from Oral Roberts University, and currently lives in Tulsa with her husband, Caleb, and their children.

more resources

Check out Sarah's other book

awake

Coming February 2021 at
sarahwehrli.com

"Awake is a message for the Body of Christ. God wants us to awaken out of
our slumber, to our purpose and mission on this earth!"
Christine Caine—Author & Speaker, Founder of A21 & Propel Women

awake

RISE TO YOUR DIVINE ASSIGNMENT

SARAH WEHRLI

Updated book and online Masterclass coming February 2021

stay connected

 pastorsarahwehrli   sarahwehrli   sarahwehrli

 sarahwehrli.com
 inspireintl.com   info@inspireintl.com   Sarah Wehrli

---

request an event

Sarah would love to consider joining you for your next event.
Here are events that she's successfully partnered with:

Women's Events
Conferences
Weekend services
Workshops
Online Events
Retreats & more

For event inquiries or any other questions, contact info@inspireintl.com.

Evangelize the Lost

Encourage People

Equip Leaders

inspireintl.com

our mission

The heart of Inspire International is to evangelize the lost, encourage people and equip leaders. Through the building of children's homes, water wells, gift distribution, women's conferences, evangelistic outreaches, and leadership training sessions, Inspire is helping reaching the world with the Gospel of Jesus.